Credit Scoring: The Ten Tools

Sponsored by:

Ezbob

The covid-19 pandemic has changed the world in so many ways. One of them is how to evaluate the creditworthiness of consumers and businesses after a period of unparalleled stress. The tried-and-true ways are unable to provide the level of insight needed in a changed world. Ezbob provides the financial services industry with a cloud platform that offers some of the most innovative lending and risk analytics, which delivers precision credit decisioning so personalised loan facilities can be offered within minutes.

We have sponsored this book because we believe that everyone involved with lending must understand the key drivers of lending decisioning. This book provides you with the knowledge needed to better manage your business.

OPOS

Opos Limited is proud to be a sponsor of this landmark risk management publication.

Opos is a leading provider of debt collection and BPO services in the banking, utility, telecoms and retail finance sectors. We provide consumer and commercial collections expertise from our state of the art service centre in West Dunbartonshire. www.oposlimited.com/opos is a FCA regulated Collections and Customer Experience service provider. This offering is further complemented by its sister company www.kapamacredit.com (debt purchase) and www.ddisoftware.co.uk (customer engagement/CRM and telephony software).

The focus on Our People and Our Systems allows us to supply quality contact centre services under both the Opos brand or in a "White Label" offering under our clients' brand. We are members of the Credit Services Association, founding members of the Scottish Compliance Forum and we hold ISO Standards; 27001, 9001 and 14001.

Credit Scoring: The Ten Tools

MURRAY L BAILEY

Trademarks

Many words in this publication that the authors and publisher believe to be trademarks, have been designated as such by use of initial capital letters. In so designating or failing to designate such words, neither the authors nor the publisher intends to express any judgment on the validity or legal status of any proprietary right that may be claimed in the words.

Published by WhiteBox an imprint of
Heritage Books Publishing

CONTENTS

i

CONTENTS

THE TEN TOOLS

.

THE TEN TOOLS

FOREWORD

From the very beginnings of my career in Credit Risk, I found myself immersed into the importance of Credit Scoring. It wasn't just about the fascinating mathematics of the models, but also about many practical considerations, not least of which is the acceptability of the scorecards to the business. Do they deliver the desired results? Are they understood? Will they last, and be robust in the face of Marketing and Operational activity? Is there anything we can learn from the models to help guide the business? I learned the need to monitor scorecards, and to ensure they really deliver what they promise, and how to identify any early problems and fix them. Most critically, I came to understand that the way in which the business uses a scorecard is usually more important than the statistics that make up that model.

When I started almost 30 years ago, scoring was just becoming widely accepted. Since then the data and computing power have grown exponentially and the modelling techniques have progressed from regression to include more advanced forms of machine learning. These are exciting times as new approaches continue to develop rapidly. There is however one constant: once a model is deployed, the fundamentals of tracking and application remain the same.

Murray Bailey has been building scorecards since the mid-1980s and launched a series of Credit Academy training courses 20 years ago. One of these popular courses was called The Ten Tools of Credit Scoring and is the foundation of this book. Just like his courses, it is full of stories and helpful tips - as well as the ten tools.

I hope that you find the book useful and enjoy success in your Credit Risk career.

Kind Regards

Jonathan Baum
Chief Credit Officer Lloyds Banking Group
April 2020

1

An Introduction to Credit Scoring

The History

People often attribute the invention of credit scoring to Fair Isaac in the mid-1950s, however it really began over a decade earlier. In 1941, in a project conducted for the US National Bureau of Economic Research, a man called David Durand studied the characteristics of Good and Bad borrowers. He obtained data from two Chicago, Illinois based firms: Spiegel Mail Order and Household Finance Corp.

I'm aware of the latter having worked for HFC in the UK and heard the story. The scorecard was not the traditional scorecard we might think of today. It was a probability model that forecast the likelihood of write-off. The model had a series of multiplicative components and required huge computing power to run. And therein lay the problem. When the model was delivered to HFC, the obvious question was: how do we deploy it? They couldn't and so the spark of the credit scoring concept failed to ignite.

The revolution came in 1956 when two mathematicians, Bill Fair and Earl Isaac formed their now famous company. They understood that the models needed to be practical and in a world where computing power was in its infancy, scorecards needed to be calculable by humans. Which fundamentally meant that instead of multiplying probabilities as Durand had done, the scores needed to be integers and additive. Using a simple mathematical conversion they built the first successful models, deployed for the American Investment Corporation (AIC) of Illinois.

Question	Answer 1	Answer 2	Answer 3	Answer 4	Answer 5	Score
Applicant's Age	<34 **15**	34-39 **19**	40-49 **20**	50 plus **29**		
Residential Status	Owner **51**	Tenant **15**	Other **21**			
Years at address	<6 **15**	6-7 **18**	8-10 **20**	> 10 **25**		
Home Phone	Yes **30**	No **15**	N/A **15**			
Occupation	Prof/ Manager **25**	H'maker / Skilled **20**	Sales/ Driver **18**	Other **15**		
Partner's Occupation	None/ Home-maker **15**	Trade/ Sales **22**	Skilled/ Manager **24**	Prof/ Retired **26**	Other **21**	
Years in Job	<1 **16**	1-7.5 **17**	7.6-15.5 **34**	> 15.5 Retired **40**	Home-maker **19**	
Bank	Major Bank **29**	Building Society **25**	Other **16**	N/A **15**		
Credit Cards	Yes **30**	No **15**				

Figure 1.1 An early scorecard

Figure 1.1 shows an early scorecard for a credit card. A customer services representative would review a paper application form and note down the points associated with certain questions. They would then add up the final column and compare this with a cut-off score. If the applicant achieved the cut-off score or better, they were accepted. If not, they were declined.

The scorecard in Figure 1.1 didn't have any credit bureau related characteristics because this was in the early days of the CRAs. Policy rules were overlaid like they are today, and these included a check that the applicant could be found on the Electoral Register and had no judgments against them or were bankrupt. Affordability was also more simplistic with many companies relying on stated annual income—that wasn't then verified. How things have changed!

The second revolution in assessing the risk of applicants for credit was the sharing of the performance of credit products between the lenders. It is very unusual indeed for a lender to not rely heavily on a new applicant's credit report (but perhaps surprisingly not always) and it's likely that the credit bureau data will contribute 80% or more of the predictive power. Some companies, in addition to policy rules, KYC and affordability checks may otherwise rely 100% on the credit report.

Big data and machine learning have arguably been the third revolution in credit scoring, with the development of more complex models as the computing power and technology has caught up with the demand for ever more predictive scorecards.

3

From Simplicity to Complexity

So at the inception of scorecards, one of the main principles was that of simplicity; integer point scores that were additive. The simple approach that Fair Isaac took was to use Natural Logarithms (Ln) of Good/Bad odds rather than probabilities. This meant that functions could be added rather than multiplied to calculate an outcome based on a number of variables. This Ln of the Odds was called the Weight of Evidence (WoE) and became a 'raw score' which could be factored up into a manageable number.

Making scorecards simple also meant that underwriters could be more easily persuaded that they were making logical and consistent decisions. Later the same simplicity could be used to persuade management that in many areas scorecards could replace human intervention.

When scorecards first took hold it was in the high volume consumer credit portfolios and mail order businesses. Not surprisingly Montgomery Ward and Sears Roebuck were early entrants to the world of scorecards. Low value, high volume lenders find the cost relative to underwriting easy to justify. However, Ford Credit was also one of the first. Ford Credit started in the mid 1960's (40 years after their main rival GMAC) and with few trained underwriters found acceptance of the concept of scoring straightforward. GMAC on the other hand did not start scoring until the mid-1980's. In the UK the centralised lenders were quicker to take up scorecards. The pace of change during the 90's, with new channels and call centres, has meant that Banks and Building Societies too have found it easier to accept scoring.

4

Whilst this principle no longer applies, many scorecards continue to be built in-line with the techniques originally used in the 50's, and the rate of change has been slow until the advent of Machine Learning. Gradient Boosting in particular has been shown to yield particular benefits over the standard Logistic Regression technique of model building. Machine Learning or AI approaches in general are beginning to find favour although regulatory focus has meant that scorecards need to be explainable, fair and legal.

Most of the tools discussed in this book apply no matter which modeling technique was used. In fact, the principles of practicality and explainability probably apply even more to AI models since the complexity makes the likelihood of error even greater. A mistake sometimes made by data scientists is to think that the best scorecard delivers the greatest separation of principal sets. The truth that every head of leading understands is that the acid test of a scorecard is the true benefit: an improvement in accounts booked for the same credit risk or a reduction in credit risk for the same level of acceptance.

QUESTIONS

SAMPLE AND DEFINITIONS

- How was "Bad" determined – look at roll rates

- How good is the scorecard if Bad were defined slightly differently?

- How was the sample window selected – consider product / marketing changes and seasonality?

- How many cases were "Indeterminate"? Consider the impact if they were Goods.

- Were the Rejects sampled in the right proportion?

- How was Reject performance inferred?

QUESTIONS

CHARACTERISTICS

- Which scorecard characteristics were calculated or translated? Check the encoding

- Was the reliability of characteristics considered?

- Over the sample window, were the attributes bad rates consistent?

- Were interactions checked for?

- How were attributes grouped?

- Did any attributes have low numbers of Bads (eg less than 30)?

QUESTIONS

SCORES

- Were scores aligned appropriately?

- Are distributions provided, smoothed or based on the actual data?

- Was the Swap Set considered?

- Do the swapped cases make sense?

- Can the model be implemented as defined?

- How many decimal places make a difference / should be considered?

QUESTIONS

SCORECARD VALIDATION

- Are the statistics (eg Gini) for the Hold-out (test) group reasonably similar?

- Look at the statistics using a more recent (out-of-time) sample with performance. Is the scorecard reasonably predictive?

- Check the Population Stability Index. Is the development population reasonably similar to the current applicant population?

- Check the Score-Odds and Misalignment Indexes for the characteristics – is there any misalignment within the development sample?

- Does the progression of point scores within characteristics make sense?

2

Selecting Variables

Characteristics

A fundamental tenet of credit scoring is that independent variables can be used to predict the dependent variable. Traditionally we call those independent variables, 'Characteristics'. In other words, the characteristics of an individual (applicant) provide information about the likelihood of that individual repaying their loan, ie being Good or Bad.

What makes a good Characteristic?

The immediate answer to this question is: predictive. But is that it? Of course not. There are a number of other considerations that make the difference between a good scorecard and one that just looks good from the development statistics.

In addition to being predictive of the outcome, a scorecard characteristic should be:
- Legal
- Explainable
- Reliable
- Not subjective
- Robust over time
- Not influenced by the business

The legal requirement is straightforward. There are anti-discrimination laws that mean you can't discriminate by gender, race or religion. In some countries this also includes age. Additionally, if there are data you cannot use because of privacy or other permissions, then no matter how predictive, don't include them.

I come from the old school where characteristics in a scorecard should be intuitive. If you can't explain them, then it's possibly down to spurious information (and sometimes mistakes). I also look for logical progression in the risk. If, for example, the bad rates decrease with 'Time at address' but have a spike at say 3 years at address, this could be explained by a request for previous addresses at less than 3 years. In other words, perhaps a subset of applicants don't wish to disclose their previous address. If you can't explain it, then re-evaluate: consider dropping the variable or consider re-binning the attributes.

Data must be reliable, which generally covers the next three categories. If the characteristic is subjective, then it won't be consistently recorded. A classic example of this is 'Job title'. I knew a large company that had 56 categories and it was down to the operator to determine which category, the applicant's job fell into. There's a huge difference between a Credit

Analyst who works for an unsecured lender and a Credit Analyst assessing the Stock Market. Even if you let the applicant decide, you are still prone to interpretation and error.

Robustness is a crucial consideration regarding variables (and we'll look at this later). Consider an extreme example of where the company used to capture data and no longer request it. A more common problem is the shift in risk over time. Predictiveness changes whether it's down to the company or socio-demographic shifts. Consider telephones. In the early days of mobile phones, anyone providing a mobile number rather than a home phone number was typically higher risk. That's not true today and there are many such examples.

I've seen scorecards with variables like credit limit, where the company determines the credit limit. Clearly, this is symptom and not the cause of subsequent behaviour. Anything that could be influenced should be considered suspect. Another problem example would be deposit for a car. Where the underwriters know the impact of a certain level of deposit on acceptance, then they may influence a broker to obtain that deposit to turn a score fail into a score pass. Unfortunately since car deposits are often mostly trade in value, then this is an easily manipulated figure.

Developers should also consider the cost of the data and future viability. For example, if you know that something isn't going to be captured in the future, or the question will be fundamentally changed, then the variable can't be included in the final scorecard.

Garbage in, garbage out

The starting point of scorecard development is to obtain or at least consider as much data as possible. What should you use, what could you use? Clean it up, understand the data and make sense of it. Determine what is reliable and what might not be. The approach I use is to group the variables based on reliability (typically 4 groups). The initial modelling only includes the most reliable variables and the more suspect ones are held back—and not included unless I convince myself otherwise. An example of one I may decide, if it has not be verified, is unreliable is 'Income'.

My four groups are shown in table 2.1.

	Verified	Not-verified
Robust	Group 1	Group 2
Less robust	Group 3	Group 4

Table 2.1 Variable classification

A SHORT STORY

A motor finance company found Deposit to be highly predictive (it usual is). There was a binary score: below 15% scored zero, at or above scored 40 (the highest points in the scorecard). Underwriters soon discovered the impact of a 15% or more deposit, and if an applicant failed with a lower deposit, they would try and get at least 15%.

Seems reasonable? No, because the scorecard was built on applicants who had provided 15% deposit without influence. Fundamentally the risk of people wasn't changing if they failed and then managed to find additional deposit (which through manipulation may not be genuine).

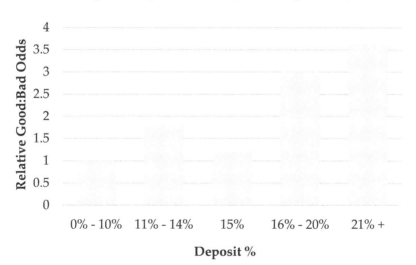

Chart showing suppressed performance for exactly 15% deposit

The Stages

The data cleansing is usually achieved by the univariate analysis. Produce a list of all of the outcomes for each variable and make sure you understand the coding especially where alpha and numeric variables are mixed. If the company used codes for certain application form entries, what do they mean? Were they consistently recorded? It may seem ridiculous, but I worked for a company that coded 'B' for home buyers and 'O' for other categories that excluded Tenants and Living with parents. However over time they changed to 'O' for Owner and Other became 'N'. Clearly, a model that was developed using Home Ownership as a characteristic could be flawed as a result.

Many scorecard developers will calculate their own variables, often augmenting the credit bureau data. But also to double check the bureau data. It's not unknown to find bureau summary codes that are incorrect! This can occur, due to error or simply because the codes may not have been calculated at the same time of the data pull. Don't just limit the calculations to the bureau data though. Some of the most interesting characteristics that I've found have been calculated. For example Engine size divided by Age for a motor finance loan.

Other calculations that I've seen include:
- Ratio of instalment to applicant's age
- Ratio of 'CAP' car valuation to loan
- Ratio of payments in the last 3 months to instalments
- Average spend over the past 6 months
- Arrears value over total outstanding credit
- Mail order credit as a percentage of total unsecured credit

Continuous variables are usually fine-classed to provide discrete outcomes and from this, variables are then binned or course-classed to yield more robust outcomes.

A word of caution in fine-classing. It may be tempting to convert all lengths of time into years, but remember my Time at address issue with 3 years at address. There may be a big difference between someone who states exactly 3 years and someone who provides more granular detail.

As a guide, consider a minimum count of 50 in each Good and Bad cell. Look for a logical progression of bad rates with the variable. As we discussed earlier, if the bad rates don't progress logically (Time at address example) then the pattern needs to be explained.

Finally, in grouping outcomes, consider the similarity of the performance using, for example, a z-test on adjacent groups (often referred to as a test for differences in proportions). Equation 2.1 shows the calculation where b is the bad rate, v is the variance and n the sample size of each group, 1 and 2.

$$z = \frac{(b_1 - b_2)}{\sqrt{(v_1 + v_2)}}$$

<u>Equation 2.1: Z-test for two groups</u>

Using the binomial approximation to estimate variance, Equation 2.1 can be made more practical by replacing the variance using the formula in Equation 2.2 for both groups 1 and 2.

$$v = \frac{b(1-b)}{n}$$

<u>Equation 2.2: Variance expressed in terms of group b</u>

So, the test for differences in proportions can be re-written as Equation 2.3, below. Where b_a is the expected average of a single distribution found using Equation 2.4.

$$Z = \frac{(b_1 - b_2)}{\sqrt{(b_a(1-b_a))(1/n_1 + 1/n_2)}}$$

<u>Equation 2.3: Test for differences in proportions</u>

$$b_a = \frac{n_1 b_1 + n_2 b_2}{n_1 + n_2}$$

<u>Equation 2.4: Average proportion of the distribution</u>

In conclusion, only by progressing carefully though character selection and construction will you avoid the "garbage out" problem. This discipline applies as much to the traditional (and slow) methods of building scorecards as it does to rapid development using machine learning. The less time spent on understanding and creating the development dataset, the more likely you are to have a scorecard that looks good, but under-performs.

EXERCISE ONE

TEST WHETHER ATTRIBUTES SHOULD BE COMBINED

Should 6 months be combined with 1 year in this example based on the z-test for differences in proportions?

Attribute	#Goods	#Bads	n	Bad rate
6 months	1831	282	2113	13.35%
1 year	951	169	1120	15.09%
Others	3322	311	3633	8.56%
Total	6104	762	6866	11.10%

Assume 95% confidence, for which z = 1.96

3

Predictive Information

Characteristics' Predictiveness

At school we learned to compare two distributions with discrete outcomes using Chi Squared. This is a test for bias between the observed result (distribution 2) and the expected (distribution 1). In doing this we propose an explanation of the problem.

In the case of potential scorecard characteristics we would propose a Null Hypothesis that there is no significant difference between the two distributions. If this test fails, then there is a significant difference.

$$X^2 = \Sigma_{(E - O)/E}$$

Equation 3.1: Chi Squared test

Equation 3.1 shows the Chi Squared test where E is the number of expected cases and O is the number observed. The calculation is summed over all outcomes and the test value can be looked up in a series of tables based on the number of degrees of freedom. Where number of degrees of freedom is the number of potential outcomes for the variable less one.

How do we know the number expected? To compare like with like, we need to assume the same total as observed. If there is no bias in the data (which is what Chi Squared is testing for) then there should be equal likelihood of any of the outcomes occurring. A common mistake with using the Chi Squared test is to use %s rather than number of cases observed, which invalidates the expected distributions and therefore test values. But there is a bigger problem. If we are using Chi Squared to compare the expected and observed, then which is which? Is Good the expected? If you do the calculation the other way round, with Bad as E, you are likely to get a different value – which could lead to a different conclusion!

A failing of Chi Squared is it doesn't compensate for how predictive an individual outcome might be and individual results can be negative, so values and cancel each other out.
Information Value (IV) on the other hand looks at the Weight of Evidence (WOE) which directly relates to risk. The combination of the two components means that the result for each outcome is positive. So there is no cancelling out. More predictive of Bad is as important as more predictive of Good.

Table 3.1 shows the Chi Squared calculation for the variable 'Residential Status'. A quick glance at the bad rates could make you suspect that this is a predictive variable. However, when we look at the calculated value it is 2.657. To determine whether to accept the Null Hypothesis that there is no bias, we need to look up the critical value for 3 degrees of freedom.

With 95% confidence we would expect a value of 7.815 or less. Since our calculated value is less than this, we would, in theory, reject this as a predictive variable.

Residential Status	#Good	#Bad	Bad Rate	Chi Sq
Owner	1323	66	5%	0.950
Renter	1198	123	9%	0.897
LWP	108	57	35%	0.472
Other	77	51	40%	0.338
Total	2706	297	10%	**2.657**

Table 3.1 Chi Squared calculation example

As we discussed in Chapter 1, the original Fair Isaac scorecards were built using Weight of Evidence (WoE), the Natural Logarithm of the proportion of Goods divided by the proportion of Bads: Ln (%G/%B). This same calculation can be used to assess the predictive power of a variable. By weighting the WoE by the difference between the proportion of Goods and Bads, we get the Information Value.

Residential Status	%Good	%Bad	%G-%B	WoE	IV
Owner	48.9%	22.2%	0.267	0.78851	0.2103
Renter	44.3%	41.4%	0.029	0.06673	0.0019
LWP	4.0%	19.2%	-0.152	-1.5704	0.2387
Other	2.8%	17.2%	-0.143	-1.7975	0.2575
Total	100.0%	100.0%			0.7084

Table 3.2 Information Value calculation example

A SHORT STORY

A lender provided guarantor and unsecured (ie non-guarantor) loans. They also had two distinct populations that we'll call Big and Small.

The challenge for the scorecard developers was that the number of Bads. Overall they were reasonable for the Logistic Regression methodology used. But by segment, the numbers highlighted the dominance of Unsecured Big.

#Bads	Unsecured	Guarantor	Total
Small	244	179	423
Big	835	372	1207
Total	1079	551	1630

Number of Bads by segment

A single scorecard was built and included the very predictive variables: Big vs Small and Unsecured vs Guarantor. However neither of these was a valid variable. Big vs Small wasn't because they were distinct populations and the scorecard was biased towards Big (lower risk) and its predictive variables. The product decision, Guarantor or not, was actually a by-product of the decision process. Applicants applied for a loan, not a product. Therefore this characteristic wouldn't be available at the decision point.

Table 3.2 shows the same example as used for the Chi Squared test. Instead of numbers of Goods and Bads, we compare the two distributions based on percentages. Unlike Chi Squared, all outcomes are positive, so something that's predictive of Bad is as important as something predicting Good. We aren't really comparing the "Goodness of Fit", we're identifying whether the Weights of Evidence might contribute to produce a powerful scorecard separating the Goods from the Bads.

The formula is shown in Equation 3.2 where %Good and %Bad refers to the proportion of Goods and Bads within their respective distributions. In this way we compare like-with-like. The calculation is for each of the attributes of a variable which is then totalled to give the Information Value of the variable.

$$I.V. = \sum(\%Goods - \%Bads) \times WoE$$

Equation 3.2: Information Value test

Unfortunately there aren't any statistical tables for Information Value, but the larger the better and by ranking the Information Values of the variables, we can determine whether one is likely to enter into a model or not.

However there is a rule of thumb, which you'll find in Tool One: Information Value.

TOOL ONE

INFORMATION VALUE

I.V. = $\sum$(%Goods - %Bads) x Weight of Evidence

Where Weight of Evidence (WoE) =

Ln (%Good/%Bad)

And where % refers to proportion so that the sum of all Goods is 100% and the sum of all Bads is 100%.

RULE OF THUMB

INFORMATION VALUE

There are no statistical tables, but scorecard developers will often consider the following as a guide.

Information Value	Interpretation
Less than 0.03	Not useful
0.03 – 0.10	Weak predictor
0.11 – 0.30	Average predictor
0.31 – 0.50	Strong predictor
Over 0.50	Very strong predictor

So less than 0.03 means that the variable is unlikely to enter into a model and may be excluded. A value of over 0.5 may mean that the variable could dominate the scorecard. This may prompt the developer to step the variable in later so that other variables (and hence more) may enter the scorecard equation.

Robustness

In most situations, the sample will be taken over a period (the Sample Window). This is done to increase the size of the sample (especially the number of Bads) and account for seasonality. However, the Bad rates may vary significantly over the window and the developer should bear this in mind when selecting the final characteristics.

For example, look at Table 3.3 which could be the numbers of Goods and Bads for the attribute "1+ cards". The Bad rate clearly fluctuates, with applications taken on in Q2, exhibiting much higher risk.

Period	Goods	Bads	Bad rate
Q1	3600	200	5.3%
Q2	2700	250	8.5%
Q3	4050	250	5.8%
Q4	4650	300	6.1%
Total.	15000	1000	6.3%

Table 3.3: Example Bad rates over a window for an attribute

We can now consider the single attribute in the same way we assessed the whole variable, where the Period effectively becomes the attribute in the Information Value calculation as shown in Equation 3.2. So the difference is that summation is over each period.

In Table 3.4, the calculation is by row with a total Robustness (R) in this example of 0.032. Since the statistic is effectively the same as Information Value we are looking at the predictiveness of a variable over time. Clearly, this isn't something we want and the rule of thumb for Robustness is similar to the rule of thumb for Information Value. However in this case a value of more than 0.03 is bad news.

Period	%Good	%Bad	%Good-%Bad	WoE	R
Q1	24%	20%	4%	0.1823	0.007
Q2	18%	25%	-7%	-0.329	0.023
Q3	27%	25%	2%	0.0770	0.002
Q4	31%	30%	1%	0.03280	0.000
Total	100%	100%			0.032

Table 3.4: Example of "Robustness"

$$\text{Robustness (R)} = \sum (\%\text{Goods} - \%\text{Bads}) \times \text{WoE}$$

Equation 3.3: Test for Robustness

An alternative test would be Chi Squared, but whichever test is used, characteristics considered within a scorecard should be checked for Robustness to consider the reliability of the variable. The higher the test value over the Sample Window, the less favoured the variable should be. The exercise in this section is for an attribute with an issue over time.

RULE OF THUMB

ROBUSTNESS

This is the Information Value test over a range of periods rather than attributes. As for I.V. there are no statistical tables, but the following is a useful guide:

Information Value	Interpretation
Less than 0.03	Not a problem
0.03 and over–	Significant variation

So a value of 0.03 or more means that the variable significantly varies in predictiveness over the Sample Window.

TIPS

ROBUSTNESS

If the Robustness Value is high, either:

- Exclude the variable, or
- Exclude abnormal periods (top and tail) from the Sample Window

EXERCISE TWO

CALCULATE THE ROBUSTNESS

The attribute "2+ dependents" has the following distribution of Bad rates by quarter opened:

Period	Goods	Bads	Bad rate
Q1	381	98	20.5%
Q2	122	22	15.3%
Q3	351	31	8.1%
Q4	465	47	9.2%
Q5	641	53	7.6%
Q6	851	61	6.7%
Q7	1044	30	2.8%
Total	3855	342	8.1%

Use the Robustness calculation to determine whether this is a problem attribute.

What might you consider if the attribute were to be retained?

4

Score Profile

Distribution

Long before we have any subsequent performance, the score distribution provides us with an early warning about whether the applicant population is significantly dissimilar from the development sample.

The first time this should be investigated is to compare the development sample to a recent sample as part of the scorecard validation. Where large samples are available, and the distribution is Normal, then a statistic testing whether the two distributions are from the same population can be used.

The formula for Divergence is shown in Equation 4.1 where SE is the average score of the expected distribution (development sample), SO is the average score of the observed (recent sample), VE is the variance in the scores for the Expected and VO is the variance for the Observed.

Since this is the measure of the difference between two Normal distributions, the standard z-test statistics will provide the critical values.

$$\text{Divergence} = \frac{(SE - SO)^2}{\frac{1}{2}\sqrt{(VE + VO)}}$$

Equation 4.1 Divergence equation

However, the assumption of Normality is fundamental and in the majority of cases, the distributions are either not Normally distributed or sample sizes are too small to make the assumption. And in credit scoring, the variation between the expected and observed for a score band can have a major implication. So for the same reason we tend not to use Chi Squared (see chapter 3), scorecard developers and analysts tend to favour a statistic that looks at the contribution at each score band.

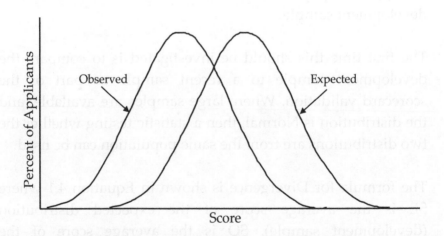

Figure 4.1 Comparing score distributions

The measure we use is the Population Stability Index, which you'll notice from Equation 4.2, looks remarkably similar to the Information Value! In this equation E and O refere to the Observed and Expected distributions, where the % is the proportion of each falling within a score band. This is summed over all of the score bands to calculate the statistic.

$$P.S.I. = \sum(\%O - \%E) \times Ln\,(\%O/\%E)$$

Equation 4.2 Population Stability Index equation

Score band	Expected Distribn	Observed Distribn	0%-E%	Ln(0%/E%)	PSI
<= 172	3.0%	2.5%	-0.5%	-18.2%	0.1%
173 - 181	4.0%	2.5%	-1.5%	-47.0%	0.7%
182 - 189	5.0%	5.5%	0.5%	9.5%	0.0%
190 - 197	3.5%	7.0%	3.5%	69.3%	2.4%
198 - 205	8.0%	4.5%	-3.5%	-57.5%	2.0%
206 - 213	8.5%	5.5%	-3.0%	-43.5%	1.3%
214 - 221	11.3%	8.0%	-3.3%	-34.5%	1.1%
222 - 229	9.6%	10.5%	0.9%	9.0%	0.1%
230 - 237	8.6%	8.8%	0.2%	2.3%	0.0%
238 - 245	11.0%	12.7%	1.7%	14.4%	0.2%
246 - 258	13.5%	17.0%	3.5%	23.1%	0.8%
>=259	14.0%	15.5%	1.5%	10.2%	0.2%
	100.0%	100.0%			9.0%

Table 4.1 Population Stability Index example

Table 4.1 provides an example. Note that the components of the PSI are always positive so that a shift in either direction indicates the variation that may be significant. Again, as with the Information Value statistic, there are no tables of critical values, however the larger the PSI, the greater the variation. As a rule of thumb, alarm bells should be ringing if the PSI is 10% or higher.

Some analysts set the Expected distribution as the recent sample prior to deployment. They then monitor the new applicants each month against this Expected. The justification might be that the original variation prior to deployment was already known and investigated. However, if the more recent application distribution varies significantly from the development sample, it is likely that the scorecard will be sub-optimal, if not erroneous. In my opinion, the Expected should always be the actual development sample distribution.

Why is a Shift Important?

Any model predicting the future relies on the assumption that the present is like the past, that nothing has changed. However, lots of things change – some more rapidly than others. Let's consider:
- Marketing
- Data collection / availability
- The competition
- Socio-demographic shifts

Marketing activity can and does bring in different applicants. This can either be deliberate or accidental. It's deliberate when Marketing target a group of prospects, perhaps directly from a database. It may be accidental if they don't appreciate that a change subsequently attracts a different profile of people. The most obvious change is pricing. A lower price will typically, on average attract a lower credit risk, higher score applicant and vice versa.

The same applies to deposit requirements where a higher deposit cuts out a sub population who can't afford the deposit. Subtle things like the creative can also draw in the right or wrong population in credit risk terms. If the proportion accepted changes then assuming all else was equal, the score distribution changed and the credit analyst should check whether it was significant enough to cause concern.

Changes to the way questions are asked – or even dropped – from an applicant can impact the assessment. For example the ordering of answers in drop down boxes can influence the selection by an applicant. The most common example of this is for Loan Purpose where it might be easy to select 'Other' or 'Consolidation'.

Similar to the Marketing impact, the competition can have a massive effect on the applicant population. Again consider interest rate. If your company had the leading interest rate, but a competitor then lowers theirs to be the cheapest, some of the people who would have applied to your company will be attracted by the competitor's product. In the modern world of comparison websites, we are extremely vulnerable to such changes. Again, if the product is perceived to become more costly, the applicant profile will fall, acceptance rates will decrease and the PSI increase.

A SHORT STORY

A new unsecured lender partnered with a retailer to offer loans to its card customers. The lender promised an acceptance rate of 80% on the basis that they would only make offers to customers with no arrears history. To make the decisions, they relied on the credit bureau score and some knock out policies. They analysed the customer base and used this to set the cut-off—based on profile of the card customers.
However, when the first applications were received, the acceptance rate was considerably lower. The applicant profile was considerably lower than expected—in other words, customers with lower scores were more likely to apply: a self-selection bias issue.

The lender interpreted this applicant profile as the "true" profile and dropped the cut-off to achieve the 80% targeted acceptance level.

Lower scores means worse performance and it was soon clear that the credit losses would be significantly higher than expected. To compensate, the lender put up prices. Which of course had two negative effects: the score profile dropped even further; and the better existing customers settled their loans, moving to lower rate competitor products.

Unsurprisingly the lender folded within two years.

The world is constantly changing. In Chapter 2 I mentioned the change in telephone ownership. This sort of thing is happening all the time and includes Credit Bureau data. For example in the UK, the risk associated with searches has changed significantly over time, first because of the growth in membership of the CRAs, then the introduction of quotation searches and the changes in the way quotation searches were available.

Because of these changes, we know that the scorecard we implement today will have a shelf life. How long, depends on the robustness of the data used and the scorecard built as well as the changes made by Marketing and the competition. In the Payday product space, performance outcomes are very short and it's easy to see the changes in populations. It's tempting to allow models to update frequently, even monthly, based on new data, however the reality is that such changes are usually too late. If the applicant population is changing so quickly, it suggests that the scorecard variables need to be more robust. We'll come back to this when talking about the power of scorecards in Chapter 9.

Accepted wisdom is that scorecards last about 3 years before they become sub-optimal. I think this is a good rule of thumb to assume that a scorecard that is more than 3 years old could be improved. However do not rely on waiting this long before evaluating whether the recent applicant population looks significantly different to the development sample by using the Population Stability Index.

TOOL TWO

POPULATION STABILITY INDEX

$$P.S.I. = \sum (\%O - \%E) \times Ln \, (\%O/\%E)$$

Where %O means the proportion (adding to 100%) of cases by score recently observed. %E is the expected distribution based on the development sample.

RULE OF THUMB

POPULATION STABILITY INDEX

Stability Index	Stability	Interpretation
Less than 10%	No change	OK
10% to 24%	Slight shift	Caution
25% and above	Shift	Danger

TIPS

POPULATION STABILITY INDEX

- Have between 10 and 20 score bands
- Try to get approximately equal percentages in each score band for the Expected distribution
- Always 'eyeball' the distribution – even if the PSI is low, a distortion may suggest a more localised problem
- Consider the type of shift
- Look for potential sub-populations.

5

Why does the type of shift matter?

The developed scorecard has a predicted Bad rate associated with each score. If the score distribution shifts, then the overall predicted risk will change as well. The type of shift shown in Figure 5.1 appears to be straight forward. The average score has increased, the standard deviation hasn't changed and so we would expect that the overall performance – the Bad rate of approved cases above the cut-off – will be lower.

This type of shift is known as a Parallel Shift and, although it may require action, it doesn't usually cause alarm regarding the scorecard. The reason for calling it a Parallel Shift is because the scores are equally shifted over the whole distribution. If the distribution were to be plotted cumulatively and on Normal distribution paper, you'd see two parallel lines.

43

The interpretation of a Positive Parallel Shift such as this is that the higher average score means a higher acceptance rate and lower credit risk. It may have been driven by positive Marketing activity, pulling in a better profile of applicant, without distorting the distribution. However the credit analyst should also consider the possibility of an external influence on characteristics such as an inflationary impact. This would be especially suspicious if the shift was gradual and trending over time.

The action could be to reduce the cut-off (if the business targets an overall rather than marginal Bad rate (see Chapter 7). However if there might be an inflationary or other impact in changing information – such as the value of certain credit bureau data – then an adjustment in the scorecard attributes may be required to bring the scores back into line.

Remember that at this stage, we typically don't have performance information and so any change should be made with caution.

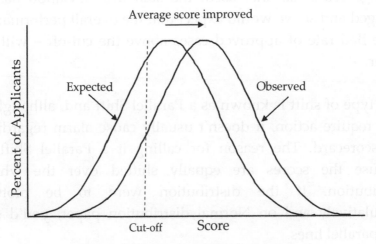

Figure 5.1 Parallel Shift example

Negative Parallel Shift

The contrary scenario is more common, where there is a negative shift in average scores (but not in the spread of scores). The average score is lower so there is a lower percentage of applicants passing the cut-off.

This is likely to mean that the overall Bad rate is higher than expected. Again it is possibly down to external influence on characteristics but may be Marketing changes (or relative changes to the competition) that has pulled in a lower profile of applicants. However, the fact that the spread of the score distribution is the same, suggests the impact is general rather than impacting a specific group (such as high or low scoring applicants).

If the cut-off was set to achieve an overall Bad rate then the solution is most likely to be to increase the cut-off. Of course this can be painful since there's a double whammy: lower acceptance means worse performance and addressing the performance issue will mean reducing acceptance even further! For this reason, it's better to identify the cause of the shift and address it holistically as a business rather than through tightening credit criteria.

Cross-over

Imagine that the scorecard distribution narrows. If the cumulative distribution was plotted on Normal distribution paper, the two lines are no longer parallel. A narrower distribution means that the distribution is narrower. This is illustrated in Figure 5.2.

Since our overall score distribution is the combination of two distributions – Good and Bad - the implication is that our Good and Bad distributions are closer than for the development sample. The overall acceptance rate and predicted Bad rates might not change, but this narrowing should concern the scorecard analyst. If our Good and Bad distributions are closer than expected then our scorecard discrimination is lower than expected. This shift is likely to result in a high Population Stability Index and suggest that a redevelopment should be investigated since the scorecard is likely to be sub-optimal.

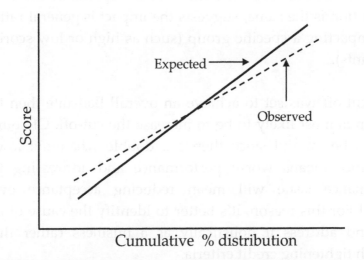

Figure 5.2 Narrow Cross-Over example

Of course the distribution could also become flatter as is illustrated by Figure 5.3. This is equally concerning. The Observed score distribution is broader than expected. At first glance one might think this is good news based on the interpretation of a Narrower Cross-Over with the suggestion that there is a greater separation of the Good and Bad distributions. Really? How could our actual experience be better than the data the scorecard was built on? It's highly unlikely.

It's possible that the original development statistics were flawed. For example was a group (like rejects) under weighted, or there's been a change in the treatment of policy declines. Note that it's best to exclude anything that isn't directly assessed by the scorecard, so exclude policy declines. So first, investigate the accuracy of the Expected score distribution. If this isn't the problem, look for sub-populations. Are there groups over or under represented between the two samples.

If a sub-population is identified and appears to be the cause of the shift, check that the scorecard works equally well for the overall and sub-population. Again, with a high Population Stability Index, it's likely that a redevelopment will be required in fairly short order.

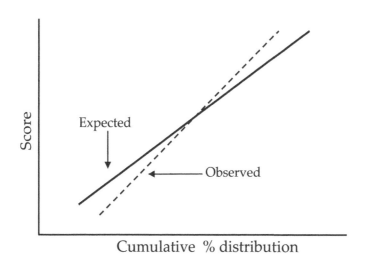

Figure 5.3 Wider Cross-Over example

Kinked Distribution

Significant Cross-Over shifts are bad news but so are non-Normal distributions when a Normal distribution was expected. Rather than get a straight line for the plot of the cumulative distribution, the result is one or more kinks in the line. Figure 5.3 illustrates how an expected Normal distribution can change to become non-Normal and when plotted cumulatively will be seen as a series of kinks.

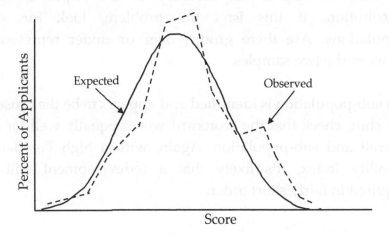

Figure 5.4 Kinked distribution example

The cause may be a partial breakdown of high point-scoring characteristics or a dominant high or low scoring sub-population. It may be due to the manipulation of applicant details either legitimately or defalcation, possibly where underwriters or an intermediary has knowledge of the scorecard and how to influence it.

If there is a sub-population present, then split the monitoring of the two groups. If the Population Stability Index is significant, then it is highly likely that a redevelopment is urgently required. You'll find the actual data for a PSI calculation as an exercise on the next page. Irrespective of the magnitude of the PSI, a distribution that looks like it has a sub population (note the peak in the high score range) should be investigated and understood.

EXERCISE THREE

CALCULATE THE PSI

Score band	Expected Distrib^n	Observed Distrib^n	O%-E%	Ln(O%/E%)	PSI
< 173	3.0%	2.5%			
173 - 181	4.0%	2.5%			
182 - 189	5.0%	5.5%			
190 - 197	3.5%	7.0%			
198 - 205	8.0%	7.5%			
206 - 213	8.5%	2.5%			
214 - 221	11.3%	8.0%			
222 - 229	9.6%	10.5%			
230 - 237	8.6%	8.8%			
238 - 245	11.0%	12.7%			
246 - 258	13.5%	17.0%			
259 +	14.0%	15.5%			
	100.0%	100.0%			

Is the shift significant and where are the concerns?

Does your opinion depend on whether the cut-off is 206 or 214?

6

Tracking scores

It is usual to track average credit scores in addition to pass rates, acceptance rates and other percentages important to the final advance rate. The average score provides an indication of a profile shift (see Chapter 5) and will directly relate to the scorecard stability if the shift is Parallel. The report that tracks this average score movement is called the Average Score Report.

Let's say that the Expected mean score of the distribution is 226.2, then tracking the Observed mean score will be another early indicator of a problem. Table 6.1 provides an example, showing that the average score difference of 7 points is of course comprised of a difference for each of the characteristics in the scorecard.

In Table 6.1 the largest variation arises from the Credit Cards characteristic, with Residential Status and Bank Type close behind. Note that the CCJ characteristic has a negative difference, demonstrating that, unlike for the Population

51

Stability Index, the Average Score Difference can mask movements in both directions. Therefore it's important for the scorecard analyst to look at the individual characteristics should they believe that the scorecard requires investigation.

Characteristic	Expected	Observed	Difference
Credit Cards	32.1	34.1	2.0
Residential Status	49.2	51.1	1.9
Time at Address	26.9	27.3	0.4
Time in Job	32.3	33.9	1.6
Bank Type	32.1	34.0	1.9
Postcode	37.4	37.8	0.4
CCJs	2.0	1.6	-0.4
Electoral Roll	14.2	13.4	-0.8
Total	226.2	233.2	7.0

Table 6.1: Example Average Score Report

Characteristic Average Score Difference

Each of the lines in Table 6.1 required a separate calculation, so let's look at Credit Cards. Table 6.2 shows each of the attributes for this scorecard characteristic and their contribution to the average score.

Now we can see the movements at an attribute level and for our Credit Cards example, the overall shift of 2 points has arisen from movements in both directions. The biggest movement is for almost 13% of applicants to have shifted from no credit card to having a card. However this receives the lowest number of points (22), so the impact on the average score is not as great as for having both types of credit card. Having a Visa and MasterCard gets 42 points and more of

52

these applicants (7.1%) has resulted in the biggest positive contribution 3%.

On the surface this may appear good news, but the scorecard analyst should always question whether this will equate to a real improvement in the performance. Three things to consider:
- Reliability of the data
- Veracity of the data
- Socio-demographic shifts

Attributes	Expected	Observed	Difference	Points	Shift
None/NA	36.0%	23.1%	-12.9%	22	-2.8
MasterCard	25.2%	20.1%	-5.1%	39	-2.0
Visa	27.6%	38.5%	10.9%	35	0.8
Visa + MC	11.2%	18.3%	7.1%	42	3.0
Total	100.0%	100.0%			2.0

Table 6.2: Example Characteristic Average Score Analysis

The first thing to note is there is an "NA" attribute. It means Not Asked or Answered. What does this mean? Is there a difference between the development sample and recent observation? It could be that previously the question wasn't mandatory and now is, or might not have been asked in all situations. If not then we aren't comparing like with like. Any increase in card ownership may be down to the capture of the question and therefore an increase in card ownership will not necessarily equate to lower credit risk.

If the question isn't validated, then it's open to misuse. In Chapter 2 we considered the selection of variables as potential scorecard characteristics. The more reliable the data, the more reliable the prediction of the Bad rate will be. If there are characteristics that aren't verified, consider a proxy for their verification. For example, there could be a check for credit cards at the credit bureau. It might not tell the company whether it's a MasterCard or Visa, but it will identify applicants claiming to have one when they don't. It might also be that they only have a pre-paid card, that appears to be a credit card but can't be found on the credit record. People who only hold pre-paid cards are unlikely to qualify for a credit card and it may be advisable to identify these separately.

An alternative approach to verification might be available within the application process. For example, the company might capture card details for repayment purposes. If this is the case, then there could be a cross-reference.

Although the Population Stability Report is a better overall early indication of a problem, drilling down into characteristics, provides insight into what is going on at an attribute level and may identify issues, particularly where the shift is Parallel and before taking remedial action.

The Importance of Score Shifts

The point scores relate to the credit risk, so a shift in scores may directly equate to a shift in the Bad rates.

Attribute	Expected Bad rate	Expected Apps	Observed Apps
None/NA	7.27%	36.0%	23.1%
MasterCard	4.25%	25.2%	20.1%
Visa	5.67%	27.6%	38.5%
Visa + MC	4.15%	11.2%	18.3%
Total	5.7%	100.0%	100.0%

Table 6.3: Example Bad rates by Attribute

Table 6.3 shows Bad rates from the development statistics associated with each attribute of the Credit Cards Characteristic. The overall Bad rate for the development population was 5.7%

Since a shift away from applicants with no credit cards, means higher average points, we can see that this equates to lower Bad rates. Using the same Expected Bad rates by Attribute, the new total Bad rate becomes 5.5%.
Note that this is not a prediction of the new outcome for the Observed applications since we haven't applied a cut-off. The same exercise can be repeated using accepted applications to predict the new Bad rate, but remember, at this stage we are still assuming that the Bad rates predicted in the scorecard development will be those observed.

We'll look at this in Chapter 13 when we consider the Characteristic Odds Report.

TOOL THREE

AVERAGE SCORE DIFFERENCE

$$\text{A.S.D.} = \Sigma(\%O - \%E) \times \text{point score}$$

Where %O means the observed proportion (adding to 100%) of cases for an attribute of a scorecard characteristic. %E is the expected proportion based on the development sample. The point score is the number of points allocated to that attribute.

RULE OF THUMB

AVERAGE SCORE DIFFERENCE

ASD*	Stability	Interpretation
Less than 3	No change	OK
3 to 5	Slight shift	Caution
Over 5 points	Shift	Danger

* Based on a scorecard where 20 points doubles the odds

TIPS

AVERAGE SCORE DIFFERENCE

- Question and investigate the reliability of the data
- Make sure you are comparing like with like (Through The Door applications vs applications)
- Remember that Characteristics' and Attribute average scores will shift in both directions and the PSI is a better overall early warning.

EXERCISE FOUR

LOOK AT THE AVERAGE SCORE DIFFERENCE

Attributes	Expected	Observed	Difference	Points	Shift
Owner	70.3%	88.3%		52	
Renter	13.0%	4.0%		43	
LWP	10.3%	1.6%		40	
Other	6.4%	6.1%		45	
Total	100.0%	100.0%			

Overall, what is the average score shift?

Are you concerned about what might be going on?

7

Cut-off Options

Lenders have an appetite for credit risk and so typically target overall Bad rate when setting a cut-off. The scorecard development output will include a prediction of risk by score. When a cut-off is considered, the Overall Bad rate it the credit risk associated with all applications at the cut-off or above. So if the company has a target Bad rate of Y, then the cut-off, from the diagram in Figure 7.1, is X.

Figure 7.2 illustrates the impact of cut-off X on the pass rate.

Note that we refer to those achieving the cut-off score as Passes rather than Accepts, since there may be other reasons for declining these applications. We'll look at such scenarios in the next section.

61

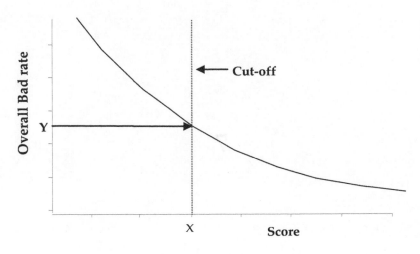

Figure 7.1: Example Bad rates by score chart

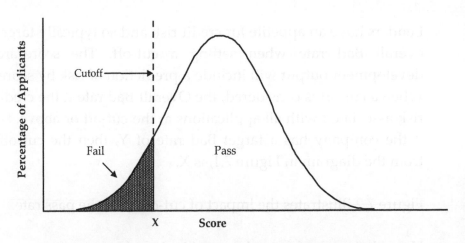

Figure 7.2: Cut-off applied to an applicant distribution

Of course, if the company has a risk appetite expressed in terms of credit loss, then a conversion needs to be considered, bearing in mind that the appetite is likely to be viewed as an annual loss percentage and the scorecard will have been developed from a sample with a finite exposure period.

Once an initial scorecard cut-off has been established, when new scorecards are implemented, the improvement looked for is typically an increase in acceptance rate for the same Bad rate. Unless, that is, the outturn of the prior scorecard was a higher credit loss than expected. In this case, improvement in Bad rate will be sort.

How do companies set the cut-off if they don't have the historical performance? Start-ups don't have the data for a bespoke scorecard, so they will either rely on a credit bureau score or purchase an expert model.

There are situations where the cut-off is set to achieve a level of acceptance rather than credit risk. Of course, the losses matter, but this often occurs where there's a relationship with a third party such as a retailer for a store card or loan that relates to their products. Since the retailer is concerned about the loss of sales (often earning far more than the commission from a credit transaction) that they may demand a minimum level of acceptance. A target acceptance rate also occurs where an intermediary has a choice of finance company - for example in car sales. If the finance company's acceptance rate falls below a threshold (official or not), then the intermediary is likely to favour another lender. For used cars, this threshold is around 50%.

Cut-offs and underwriters

Where underwriters are used in conjunction with a scorecard, there are three approaches:
- Soft cut-off
- Grey Zone
- Risk Grades

The Soft cut-off is where it is a guide and the underwriters are allowed to "cherry pick" below this score. This makes sense where a scorecard is new and untested or where there is additional information available to the underwriters, that wasn't assessed by the scorecard. Of course, allowing a small number of approvals below the cut-off also provides the credit analyst with an appreciation of the score fails.

Score fails are important for future scorecard development, since our Known population of Goods and Bads is truncated and therefor biased. A developer should consider Reject Inference to estimate the performance of the Rejects, and so any lessons from approving score fails can help with this extrapolation.

A Grey Zone is where the underwriters work a score band, below which are fails, above which are passes. The lower score can prevent underwriters from digging too deep and accepting very high risk cases. The higher cut-off can save manual effort where the credit risk is so good, that no further investigation is required.

Risk Grades are where the scores are split into sectors, possibly providing a guide for underwriters. Figure 7.3 illustrates such a system.

A SHORT STORY

An unsecured loan for a retail sector had an acceptance rate of around 55%. At the same level of risk, a new scorecard suggested an acceptance rate of 79%. The scorecard developer explained that this was due to the development sample being product specific whereas the previous model had included other retail loans. The developer refused to disclose the detail and said "Trust me" when challenged.

The actual acceptance rate was soon confirmed as down, at around 52%. What the developer had failed to appreciate was the amount of manual underwriting taking place. The underwriters were looking at information outside that available to the scorecard, not least of which was the affordability. It was a foolish mistake, that subsequently cost him his job and could have cost the business significantly.

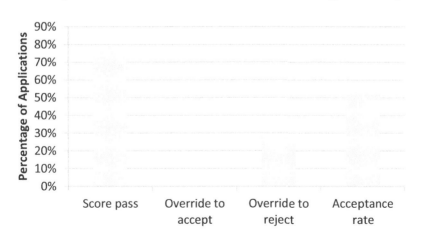

Chart showing the impact of overrides

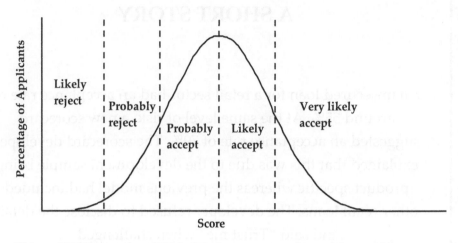

Figure 7.3: Example of Risk Grades as an underwriting guide

The problem with this becomes immediately apparent: what does "probably" mean versus "likely"? In fact, I've experienced many more categories including the words: "possibly" and "consider". It's difficult to ensure consistency between individual underwriters, with such vague terminology. And this approach tends to be limited to the motor finance and business loan sectors where reliance on the credit score is lower than other sectors.

Strategies Using Risk Grades

Risk Grades are used in many more ways than just advising underwriters on the likelihood of approval. Many organisations use them without giving them names, others think of them as categories, such as Gold, Silver and Bronze. You can have fun naming these and the most bizarre I've come across is Fruits. I understood Lemons and Cherries but just where Bananas and Oranges fit in this ranking was unclear to me.

In addition to using Risk Grades for verification checks, the most common use of these categories is for Risk Based Pricing and product features, such as credit limits for credit cards. Table 7.1 shows examples of limits and checks to be made. Note that these are not necessarily in combination and the table is just for illustrative purposes. Automated verification may be relied on for lower risk applicants. Interest rates may be lower and the amount advanced or credit limit higher.

Category	Income Checks	Interest rate	Maximum loan amount
Bronze	Bank statements	16%	£5,000
Silver	Statements or payslips	12%	£10,000
Gold	CRA verification	8%	£15,000
Platinum	CRA verification	5%	£20,000

Table 7.1: Examples of using Risk Grades

But how do we apply science to this Risk Grade approach? The problem we have is that our prediction of Bad rates (and hence credit loss) is based on our previous, modelled experience. By applying different rules to different score bands, we are effectively undermining the model. However, we don't live in a perfect world and this problem is akin to the one we experience with behavioural scoring, where it's all

67

about the best strategy rather than acceptance for the product. Test and learn is the only way to truly discover the impact of our various rules. However, it is always good to base the initial decisions on something.

Table 7.2 illustrates a Value at Risk (VaR) approach where the impact of varying credit limits is considered on the amount of money at risk. The example shows the VaR calculated by multiplying the credit limit by the Bad rate for each score band (ie Risk Grade). In this example the VaR increases with score until 170 after which it declines. The challenge for credit card companies is always to increase balances for lower risk customers and the example suggests that more risk could be taken for higher scores by increasing limits significantly.

Score band	% Approved	Bad rate	Credit Limit	VaR
<140	10%	6.0%	500	30
140 - 149	15%	5.0%	1,000	50
150 - 159	15%	4.0%	2,000	80
160 - 169	15%	3.0%	3,000	90
170 - 179	15%	2.0%	4,000	80
180 - 189	15%	1.0%	5,000	50
190 +	15%	0.5%	6,000	30
Total	100%	2.9%	3,200	60

Table 7.2: Example of VaR for credit limits

VaR relates more closely to the credit loss since it is by value rather than number of Bads. The approach can be refined by considering the likely balance of accounts, recognizing that Bad customers typically result in the write off near the credit limit, whereas Good customers may maintain much lower balances. This mix clearly has a big impact on the write-off expressed as a proportion of balances by Risk Grade.

The Expected Loss calculation used for Capital Adequacy considers the average balance of accounts reaching default, which is ideal if the information is available – although again, when testing new strategies, assumptions will need to be made.

TOOL FOUR

VALUE AT RISK

$$V.a.R. = \sum \text{Bad rate} \times \beta \times L$$

Where L is the loan amount advanced or credit limit and β is a factor to account for take-up rates or usage.

This is very similar to the Capital Adequacy calculation for Expected Loss (E.L.) where:

$$E.L. = PD \times EAD \times LGD$$

Where PD = probability of default (often synonymous with Bad rate, but not necessarily), EAD is Exposure at Default, and LGD is the Loss Given Default.

TIPS

VALUE AT RISK

- For loans, watch out for an increase in cancellations. Lower risk applicants deselect themselves as interest rates increase

- For credit limits, the loss on a Bad customer is typically close to the limit. Good customers tend to maintain much lower balances.

EXERCISE FIVE

SET THE CUT-OFF

Score band	Proportion	Descending Cumulative	Marginal Bad rate	Overall Bad rate
< 160	3%	100%	46.7%	9.8%
160 - 172	5%	97%	35.0%	8.7%
173 - 181	6%	92%	26.0%	7.2%
182 - 189	8%	86%	19.5%	5.8%
190 - 197	10%	78%	15.1%	4.4%
198 - 205	9%	68%	8.2%	2.9%
206 - 213	11%	59%	4.9%	2.1%
214 - 221	9%	48%	2.9%	1.4%
222 - 229	8%	39%	1.8%	1.1%
230 - 237	8%	31%	1.3%	0.9%
238 - 245	7%	23%	1.0%	0.7%
246 - 258	8%	16%	0.8%	0.6%
259 - 270	4%	8%	0.5%	0.4%
270+	4%	4%	0.3%	0.3%
Total	100%	100%	9.8%	9.8%

What's the recommended cut-off if:

- the target acceptance rate is 68%?
- the target overall Bad rate is 4.4%?

What if the company makes a loss when the odds fall below 11?

8

Correlation and Interaction

Regression Models

We could look at each individual variable, calculate the Weight of Evidence and convert this into a score – just like Fair Isaac did with their first scorecards. But they then used a technique called "Iterative Search" to find the best weights for the scorecard. Why did they do this? Because most of the variables will be correlated. The overlap of information can be significant and can therefore provide a model that wouldn't be as powerful as predicted. See the Short Story in this chapter for a real-life example. Figure 8.1 illustrates the overlap of information provided by the variables Age and Time at Address.

Most scorecard models rely on multiple regression to identify this overlap, or correlation, using the probability of Good as the predictor. The solid line in figure 9.4 demonstrates Ordinary Least Squares (OLS) regression; the 'line of best fit' between variables.

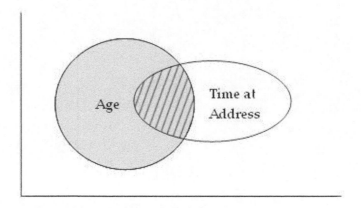

Figure 8.2: Illustration of correlation

For linear regression the scorecard equation is shown in Equation 8.1, where β is the correlation coefficient of variable x and c is a constant. OLS requires data to be continuous and Normal. Since these requirements are likely to be violated one could argue that this modelling approach should not be used. However, OLS is often used in favour of more advanced methods due to simplicity and the ease with which it can be explained.

$$Risk = \sum \beta x + c$$

Equation 8.1: The linear regression equation

Figure 8.2 illustrates a linear relationship between the dependent variable (Risk) and an independent variable x. OLS minimizes the error between the prediction and the observation. For Equation 8.2, if yo is the true risk of the observed case, yp is the predicted risk according to the equation and ym is the mean risk, then SSR is the sum of the squares of the residual (yo – yp) and SST is the sum of the squares to the observation (yo – ym).

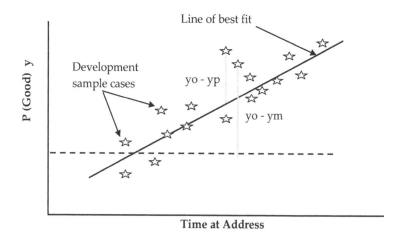

Figure 8.2: Illustration of OLS line of best fit

$$R^2 = 1 - SSR / SST$$

Equation 8.2: The linear regression equation

However, looking at Figure 8.2, one can immediately see the issue. The P(Good) we observe is binary and not linear, so although linear regression works, it's by no means optimal.

A rule of thumb introduced many years ago, by Fair Isaac was that there should be at least 1,500 Goods, 1,500 Bads and 1,500 Rejects for a robust model build. Developers now use this guide to determine when Logistic regression may be used rather than an OLS approach. Logistic regression provides a probabilistic solution, more in keeping with the modelling of Good or Bad rates and produces a better scorecard where sample sizes are reasonable.

The scorecard equation is illustrated in Equation 8.2. Here P(Good) is the probability of a Good outcome and 'Exp' is the exponential function.

$$P(Good) \ = \ \frac{Exp(\Sigma \ \beta x + c)}{1 + Exp(\Sigma \ \beta x + c)}$$

Equation 8.3: The logistic regression equation

Interaction

The assumption of regression is that the line of best fit is independent of any interaction between the variables. In other words it is consistent for the whole variable, irrespective of the relationship with the other variable. What we are modelling using any regression technique is the average fit.

Consider Figure 8.3 which shows that the overlap of information between variables might not be the same as the correlation for each individual variable. Here we see that Owners tend to be lower risk for Older customers but higher risk for younger ones. This situation occurs where young people overstretch themselves with mortgage payments and may have higher LTVs. We'll see later that more information may unpick this interaction, but for the Linear and Logistic regression approaches to scorecard modelling, it's a major issue.

76

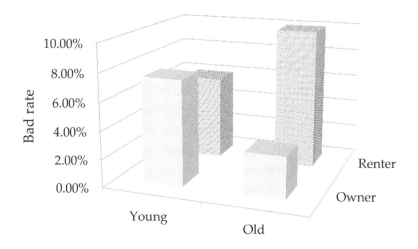

Figure 8.3: Example risk by two variables

Identifying Interaction

Experienced developers know what to look for since these interactions are common across populations. But a recognized technique is to use CHAID to identify whether there is likely to be interaction between key variables.

CHAID builds a decision tree using Chi Squared to identify splits (see Chapter 3 for a discussion of Chi Squared vs Information Value). Figure 8.4 illustrates a resulting tree (to two levels) where the pattern of selected variables changes. From this we can see that there's a different pattern emerging from the initial split based on Age. The next most predictive (according to Chi Squared) is Credit Cards for Young people compared to the Older group's residential status.

Note that there are Information Value alternatives to CHAID available and C5.0, for example, will provide splits that are

77

directly related to the Weight of Evidence and is arguably more useful within scorecard development.

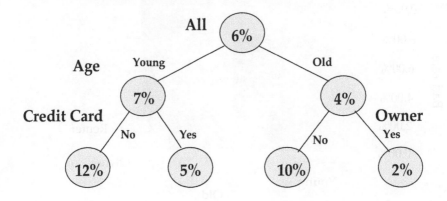

Figure 8.4 CHAID tree example

Dealing with Interactions

There are three approaches worthy of mention:
- Combined variables
- Multiple scorecards
- Alternative modelling technique

If there is an interaction between Age and Residential status, then a straightforward solution is to build a new two-dimensional variable so that we can look at Young Owners and Old Owners, and their contribution to the prediction of risk, separately. The limitation is usually the amount of data, but this can be taken down to three levels, such as Young Owners with a credit card. However with many years' experience, even modelling vast numbers of payday loans has only rarely thrown such multi-layered variables into the final scorecard.

If the pattern of predictive variables thrown up by CHAID or a similar technique varies significantly (ie for multiple variables) then multiple scorecards will yield better discrimination overall and confining the variables to a single regression-based scorecard will be sub-optimal. Again the main limitation is volume of data.

Which leads us onto the third alternative. If there is enough data (suggested as tens of thousands of cases) then a more advanced technique can be used. Historically neural networks were favoured since they effectively built multiple models within one. Random Forests rose to the fore in the last decade, but more recent developments in machine learning and computing power has led to Gradient Boosting as a popular technique. It has yet to find widespread acceptance, not least due to the old issue of explainability.

A SHORT STORY

A retail credit card company had a scorecard built by an analyst without a statistical background. He'd attended a training course and understood the principle of using odds to build a scorecard and knew that the Weight of Evidence provided a raw score. The applicant population looked like the chart shown below. The analyst explained the two humps as being a demonstration of the predictiveness of the scorecard – the left hand hump related to the Bads and the right hand one the Goods.

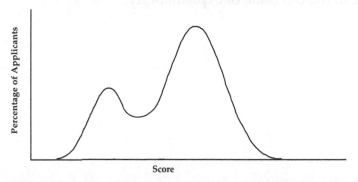

Chart showing the profile of recent applications

What he'd done was to take the 7 most predictive variables, calculate the WoE for each of their attributes and then scale the decimal into an integer. Of course he'd ignored the correlation between these variables by taking each at their full value. When the population was analysed it became clear that the hump on the left was associated with younger applicants who, while being higher risk generally, became penalised by most of the characteristics.

TOOL FIVE

INTERACTION INDEX

Interaction Index $= \mathrm{Ln}\,(O_{11} \times O_{22} / O_{12} \times O_{21})$

Where O_{ii} are the Good: Bad Odds for each cell of a two by two matrix of one variable (x) vs another (y) and where the outcome is binary (1,0).

Odds	Variable y - 1	Variable y - 0
Variable x - 1	O_{11}	O_{12}
Variable x - 0	O_{21}	O_{22}

RULE OF THUMB

INTERACTION INDEX

Interaction Index	Action
< -0.5	Investigate
-0.5 to 0.5	None
> 0.5	Investigate

9

Scorecard Predictiveness

Scorecard Statistics

In Chapter 8 we looked the regression equation and R Squared. R Squared is not a direct measure of how predictive the scorecard is, it's a measure of how close a fit the predictive line is versus the actual development data points. A better R Squared does not imply a better separation of Goods and Bads, but a low value will indicate that the predicted relationship is weak.

In Chapter 4 we looked at Divergence as a measure of the difference between the Observed and Expected applicant distributions. This statistic was one of the first used to determine the predictiveness of scorecards, looking at the Good versus the Bad distributions. Another simple statistic used is Kolmagorov-Smirnov or K-S test. Figure 9.1 shows the cumulative distributions, Good and Bad. The K-S is the maximum separation of the two lines.

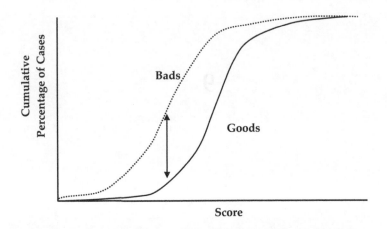

Figure 9.1 Graph illustrating the K-S test statistic

There are statistical tables with critical values for K-S, however with only small numbers (a few hundred cases), a small K-S is significant and it really just tells us that the two populations are different. The problem with Divergence was that the distributions should be Normal and not too dissimilar in terms of spread. The issue with K-S is that it tells us nothing about the rest of the distribution. If the curve is all over the place, the maximum separation can be misleading.

The Gini Index (or Coefficient) considers whole distribution and has therefore found more favour in the industry for identifying how well a model discriminates between Goods and Bads. Referring to Figure 9.2, the Cumulative distribution of the Goods is plotted against the cumulative distribution of the Bads. The diagonal, dashed line represents the line of no discrimination whereas the curve is the scorecard prediction with more of the Bads arising before the Goods. For example at the point market "a", there are 50% of the Bads at this score or below, but only about 12% of the Goods.

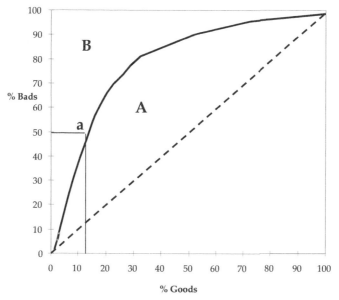

Figure 9.2. Gini diagram

The Gini Index is calculated as the area between the scorecard line and the line of no discrimination as a percentage of the triangle A+B ie the Gini is the area A/(A+B). The result will be between 0% and 100%, with 0% representing a random decision process and 100% representing prefect discrimination where the Good and Bads are completed separated.

A similar metric is commonly used called Area Under Receiver Operating Characteristic although more commonly shortened to AUC. Equation 9.1 is the conversion of an AUC to the Gini.

A SHORT STORY

A large motor finance company had a batch of frauds and with around 50 confirmed frauds, attempted and failed to build a scorecard that provided a reasonable False:Positive rate. The best Gini Index they could achieve was 43%, but looking at the worst scoring 20%, still only yielded under 40% of the frauds.

A company specialising in Neural Networks happened to be doing some other work for the company and offered to look at the fraud problem. Very quickly the reported great success with a Gini Index of almost 90%. They also managed to find 65% of the frauds in the bottom 20% of the cases.

There was no Hold-out sample (no test population) since there were so few frauds. However, there were recent applications that could be assessed against the new model. The shocking result was that no clear frauds were identified in the highest risk groups. When the model was analysed, the company discovered that the modellers had used the identifier of the car salesman responsible for the credit sale. This was the most predictive factor. The motor finance company already knew this and had taken action against the employees. The model was useless and never implemented.

The lesson is that a high Gini should always suggest over-fitting – especially when the sample of Bads (frauds in this case) is small.

$$\text{Gini} = 2 \times \text{AUC} - 1$$

<u>Equation 9.1: Relationship between Gini and AUC</u>

Counting Flips

Another way of thinking about or explaining the Gini Index is to consider "Flips". If the cases (Good and Bad) are considered in pairs, how many times do they have to exchange places to either result in a perfectly random model (the Null or no discrimination, dotted line in Figure 9.2) and the number that results in all the Bads followed by all the Goods, in other words a perfect scorecard.

$$\text{Gini} = 1 - \text{Flips to Perfect} / \text{Flips Null to Perfect}$$

<u>Equation 9.2: Gini expressed as Flips</u>

Let's consider a scorecard made up of 20 cases: ten Goods (G) and ten Bads (B).

B B G B G B B G B G G G

Null would be:
B G B G B G B G B G B G

Perfect would be:
B B B B B B G G G G G G

The Gini formula based on Flips is shown in Equation 9.2. Using our example above, Null to perfect would require 15 Flips (ie 1 + 2 + 3 + 4 + 5). Our scorecard is better than this and requires 8 Flips (ie 1 + 3 + 4). So the Gini for our simple example is 46.7% (ie 1 – 8/15).

What's a Good Gini?

It depends. Scorecards for credit application populations typically have Gini Indexes of between 60% and 80%, but it depends very much on the product and segment. For example a product aimed at young people will have less history or depth of information (especially credit bureau data) to assess and a scorecard development may only yield a model with say 30%. This is still better than no discrimination of course and the test is often that a new model delivers greater discrimination than a previous one. So the higher the Gini the better.

What it doesn't tell us however, is whether the scorecard has achieved a higher Gini because it has over-fit the data or what real benefit the scorecard will deliver the business. What really matters is the acceptance rate versus the Bad rate. A scorecard with a higher Gini is no benefit if the Bad rate is worse for the same level of acceptance.

To address the over-fitting concern, developer usually have a Hold-out sample. Having built a model, they will then test this model against the sample not modelled and look for a similar set of results, not least of which will be the Gini coefficient. As a rule of thumb, a difference of more than 5% suggests there has been over-fitting.

The problem often arises that the development sample wasn't large enough to justify a Hold-out group – or the Hold-out group is so small that large statistical variations will be expected and observed. A solution to this is to develop on the full sample and then test it against multiple smaller samples within the population rather than have a Hold-out group.

Confusion

A Confusion Matrix is a comparison of the predicted and actual values for a given cut-off (or Threshold) Figure 9.3 provides an example showing a matrix of the number of cases where the threshold is set to achieve the same Bad rate, and where:

- The model predicted Bad and the case was defined as Bad — ie True Positive (TP)
- The model predicted a Bad and the case was Good — ie False Positive (FP)
- The model predicted Good and the case was Good — ie True Negative (TN)
- The model predicted no Bad and the case was Bad — ie False Negative (FN)

		Actual	
		Bad	Good
Predicted	Bad	512	315
	Good	315	2978

Figure 9.3: Example Confusion Martix

So our model predicted that 315 of our Bad cases would turn out Good. This can be expressed as a False Positive Rate (FPR) of all Goods. Using the equation in Equation 9.3 and the figures from our example in Figure 9.3, the False Positive Rate is 315 / (315 + 2978) = 9.6%. ie our model has misclassified almost 10% of the Goods.

$$FPR = FP / (FP + TN)$$

Equation 9.3: False Positive Rate

We can also look at the degree our model has accurately classified Bads at this cut-off. Using the formula in Equation 9.4, the True Positive Rate is 62% ie 512 / (512 + 315).

$$TPR = TP / (TP + FN)$$

Equation 9.4: False Positive Rate

Note that the Gini curve (officially known as the ROC curve) is constructed by using Confusion Matrices from all individual and driving their TPR and FPR. The y-axis of the ROC curve represents the TPR values, and the x-axis represents the FPR values.

TOOL SIX

GINI INDEX

$$Gini = A / (A + B) = 2A$$

Where A is the area between the predicted line and the null
line and A + B is the area of the triangle (ie ½)

Which is approximately

$$Gini = 1 - (Within + Between)$$

Where "Within" $= \Sigma(B_i \times G_i)$
and "Between" $= 2\Sigma(B_i \times CG_{i-1})$

Where G_i and B_i are the proportion of the Goods and Bads at
score i and CG_{i-1} is cumulative proportion of Goods up to the
previous score band.

RULE OF THUMB

GINI INDEX

The rule for a new scorecard is that the new Gini should be better than the old rather than there be an absolute value that is acceptable.

However when comparing scorecards, especially where there is a Test or Hold-out sample, consider:

Difference in Gini	Action
< 5%	None
>= 5%	Investigate whether improvement is genuine

EXERCISE SIX

CALCULATE THE GINI INDEX

%Gi	%Bi	CGi	Within	Between
0%	1%	0%		
1%	2%	1%		
2%	2%	3%		
2%	3%	5%		
2%	4%	7%		
2%	5%	9%		
2%	6%	11%		
2%	6%	13%		
3%	8%	16%		
3%	8%	19%		
3%	10%	22%		
3%	11%	25%		
4%	10%	29%		
4%	8%	33%		
5%	5%	38%		
8%	2%	46%		
10%	2%	56%		
11%	2%	67%		
9%	2%	76%		
10%	2%	86%		
14%	1%	100%		
		Total		

Use the formula:

Gini = 100% - (Within% + Between%)

10

Understanding improvements

In Chapter 9 we considered statistics that tell us about a scorecard's predictiveness. We finished by considering the Confusion Matrix. This matrix tells us how well the model has fit the data, but what it hasn't told us is how well this scorecard compares to the previous situation. The statistics may indicate a better scorecard, but what has it done to achieve this improvement?

The best way to consider what's going on is the Swap Set. Figure 10.1 illustrates the swap over that should be achieved by an improved scorecard. Previous Bad Accepts become rejected and Previous Good Declines are accepted.

Any cut-off can be considered, and it's common to look at the ones that yield the same acceptance rate. Table 10.1 shows an example of a Swap Set when the old and new scorecard

95

decisions are compared. 5% of previous Rejects have become Accepts and vice versa. This is where the improvement has come from.

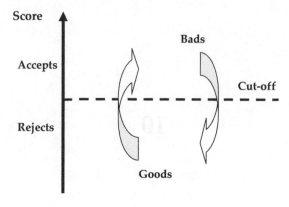

Figure 10.1: Swap caused by an improved scorecard

		Old scorecard	
		Accept	Reject
New scorecard	Accept	75%	5%
	Reject	5%	15%

Table 10.1: Swap set matrix example

However, Table 10.1 doesn't tell us what we really need to know: what happened to the Goods and Bads? So a better Swap Set analysis would be for each principal set independently. Table 10.2 shows the matrix for Good alone where Good A means accepted Good cases and Good R means rejected Good cases. The new scorecard should show that more Goods move from being previously rejected to previously accepted.

		Old scorecard	
		Good A	Good R
New scorecard	Good A	85%	7%
	Good R	3%	5%

Table 10.2: Swap set matrix example for Goods

Underwriting

Things are rarely straightforward and, where used, underwriters and policy rules will have an impact on the past and future decisions using any scorecard.

Let's look at an example. If the previous rejection rate was 44%, but the score fail rate was only 21.5%, therefore other decision making is having a significant impact and must be considered in the process of determining whether a new scorecard is better. Note that the short story from Chapter 7 also applies here.

In Table 10.3, the Swap Set is 6.5% from Pass to Fail and, maintaining the same acceptance rate, 6.5% goes from Fail to Pass. However 27% go from Reject to Pass which would appear to offer huge opportunity. But looking closer we see that most of these (21.5% of applications) passed the previous scorecard cut-off. The question that the scorecard analyst must therefore ask is what will happen to these cases. What will Underwriting do after the new scorecard is deployed?

Old Scorecard	Old decision	New scorecard	%
Fail	Reject	Fail	14.0%
Pass	Reject	Fail	3.0%
Fail	Accept	Fail	1.0%
Pass	Accept	Fail	3.5%
Fail	Reject	Pass	5.5%
Pass	Reject	Pass	21.5%
Fail	Accept	Pass	1.0%
Pass	Accept	Pass	50.5%

Table 10.3: 3D Swap set matrix example

The best way to assess what will really happen is to sample the Swap Set cases. Look at the detail and try to determine whether a Pass/Reject should still be rejected or whether the policy rules or underwriting needs to be re-evaluated. The most difficult group to assess are the ones that underwriting probably never saw before and may be the source of any really improvement. These are the Fail-Reject-Pass (F-R-P) cases. In Table 10.3 these make up 5.5% of the applications.

Continuing with the abbreviation Old scorecard decision – Underwriter decision – New Scorecard decision, Table 10:4 describes the type of swap of each category. The F-R-F and P-A-P categories are the extremes where the both scorecards and underwriters agree. Then there are the groups where the new scorecard agrees with the underwriters who previously overrode the scorecard. Then there are the overrides where the new scorecard continues to agree with the old one (F-A-F and P-R-P). Unless a policy change is made, it is likely that the underwriters will continue to override these. In the example above (Table 10.3) the P-R-P is clearly a significant group and the scorecard analyst needs to understand what is going on here. What is the scorecard missing and can this be better managed by rejecting application automatically rather than rely on the judgement of Underwriting.

Type	Interpretation	New decision
F-R-F	Confirmation	Reject
P-R-F	Agreed Swap	Reject
F-A-F	Lowside Override	Accept?
P-A-F	Decision Swap	Reject
F-R-P	Decision Swap	Accept
P-R-P	Highside Override	Reject?
F-A-P	Agreed Swap	Accept
P-A-P	Confirmation	Accept

Table 10.4: 3D Swap set matrix interpretation

The Decision Swap groups (P-A-F and F-R-P) are where the real benefit is likely to result from the new scorecard. Table 10.4 shows the assumption that the underwriters will agree with the swaps, however a review of cases is advisable since the new scorecard could be undermined by the rejection of a significant proportion of F-R-Ps. Note that it is unlikely that this latter group received much attention from Underwriting in the past.

EXERCISE SEVEN

CALCULATE THE SWAP SET

Old Scorecard	Old decision	New scorecard	%	New decision
Fail	Reject	Fail	10%	
Pass	Reject	Fail	7%	
Fail	Accept	Fail	1%	
Pass	Accept	Fail	4%	
Fail	Reject	Pass	8%	
Pass	Reject	Pass	5%	
Fail	Accept	Pass	5%	
Pass	Accept	Pass	60%	

Just looking at Pass and Fail, what is the Swap Set percentage?

The old Reject rate was 30%. Predict what the new Reject rate will be.

A SHORT STORY

An unsecured loan company had a system whereby applicants were either offered a Secured (SEC) or Unsecured loan. The former was offered where the risk was considered too high. Although the number of Bads was below a thousand, a scorecard was subsequently built using the unsecured loans alone. The risk of the accounts declined for this product (offered SEC loans) was then considered and used to augment the final model. After a number of iterations to limit over-fitting the resulting scorecard had a paltry Gini of 34%. However, using a CRA score achieved only 20%, so this was a vast improvement.

On the other hand, the business used Risk Grades (A to D) and had approved too many of the higher risk D cases. The new scorecard didn't address this, so different developers were used and they achieved the target level of Ds and a 54% Gini. However, they included the SEC loans as though they had been unsecured. The problem with this is that the SEC loan applicants should have been higher risk but performed better because of the SEC (there was also a high degree of self-selection with over 90% offered a SEC loan not proceeding). The final scorecard may have had a higher Gini and achieved an acceptable level of Ds, but this is a fool's errand.

Any model assumes the future is like the past and those applicants now getting an unsecured loan where they had received a SEC loan in the past, will not perform as predicted.

Reject Inference

Since the improvement of a scorecard typically comes from approving previous rejects that we think were misclassified, then the treatment of previous Rejects in the scorecard modelling process is critical.

Table 10.5 provides an example of the Gini Indexes calculated using different approaches to reject Inference.

	Known GB	RI 1	RI 2
Gini	39.50%	43.20%	45.50%

Table 10.5: Example of impact of RI on Gini

In Table 10.5, "Known GB", is the sample of Good and Bads with actual known performance. This is compared with two Reject Inference (RI) approaches where RI 2 is based on assuming all Rejects are Bad. This is an extreme position to take and would only make sense if the company only wanted to tighten scores and reject more applicants who look like previous Rejects. However it demonstrates that Reject Inference is likely to produce a larger Gini Index and the more extreme the treatment, the larger the separation between Goods and Bads will be.

The reason for showing this is to highlight the need to understand what Reject Inference technique was used, but also to review cases afterwards to ensure that the predicted performance looks reasonable. This is why the Swap Set analysis is so important in the process of approving a new scorecard.

Information on how developers can "cheat" during the credit scorecard development process, which includes Reject Inference, can be found in the book entitled: "Credit Scoring: The Principles and Practicalities".

QUESTIONS TO ASK:

REJECT INFERENCE

- What, if any, Reject Inference (RI) technique was used?

- What impact did the RI have on improvements?

  - How were policy and overrides treated?

    - 'Policies' should be excluded

  - If overrides significant, look at distribution

    - Compare the Characteristic Analyses of Accepts vs Rejects (AR)

- Were Characteristics with AR Information Values > 0.5 considered?

  - Are there any potential policy decline rules?

- What would be the impact if all previous Rejects were treated as Bad?

TOOL SEVEN

SWAP SET ANALYSIS

		Old scorecard	
		Accept	Reject
New scorecard	Accept	AA	AR
	Reject	RA	RR

The Swap Set is RA and AR where the benefit comes from accepting Goods, previously rejected and declining Bads previously accepted.

For a given cut-off the total Swap Set is RA + AR

TIPS

SWAP SET ANALYSIS

- Beware swaps of more than 10%

- Take policy declines out of the analysis

- Watch for the impact of Underwriting

- Check the Swap Set for Goods and split between Known and Inferred.

11

Account Performance

Performance over time

The first thing we look at is the quality of new business. The acceptance rate compared to what we expected and the score distribution. In Chapter 4 we looked at the Population Stability Index which is our first early indicator of whether things are as expected. Once we have repayment performance, however, we have a much better guide as to whether the scorecard is delivering the expected result.

Scorecards predict a Bad rate at a point in time and so we need to track vintages of accounts, looking at performance by exposure. Figure 11.1 is an example Vintage Analysis Report, showing each vintage or cohort of accounts and the Bad rate outcome each period. For simplicity the example shows quarters of business observed every 3 months. Most companies do this month by month, however sample size may make such granularity unreliable, so the advice is to consider statistical error and if a single month doesn't constrain the error to an acceptable level, then track quarters – or even wider periods. The figures in Figure 11.1 are the number of Bads divided by the number of loans advanced or accounts opened.

		Quarter Exposure Observed						
		Q1	Q2	Q3	Q4	Q5	Q6	Q7
Quarter Advanced	Q1'19	0.65	1.39	2.59	3.43	3.92	4.08	4.12
	Q2'19	0.74	1.48	2.65	3.36	3.62	3.71	3.73
	Q3'19	0.61	1.27	2.55	3.31	3.87	4.06	
	Q4'19	0.91	1.79	3.23	4.20	4.77		
	Q1'20	0.73	1.47	2.86	3.71			
	Q2'20	0.82	1.67	3.21				
	Q3'20	0.63	1.60					
	Q4'20	0.88						

Figure 11.1: Example Vintage Analysis Report

For reference, the 95% confidence test assuming a Normal distribution of Bad rate results is provided as Equation 11.1, where B is the Bad rate and N is the sample size.

$$\text{Error} = 1.96 \times \sqrt{(B\% \, (100\text{-}B\%)/N)}$$

Equation 11.1: Binomial approximation for the 95% Confidence Interval

Note that for portfolio management, businesses often track the value of arrears within vintage reports. The purpose of this is very different to scorecard tracking, where we are comparing the outturn with the Bad rate predicted by the scorecard. As we saw in Chapter 4, this Bad rate will depend on the score profile, so it is usual to include the expected Bad rate for each period comparative purposes.

Gini Over Time

It's worth noting that there are other metrics used to track the performance of a scorecard. If Gini was used in the original assessment of a scorecard, it may be tracked over time based on the performance of cases observed.

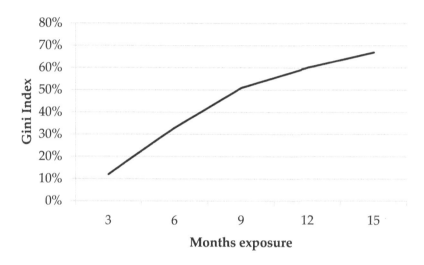

Figure 11.2: Example of tracking Gini over time

Note that the Gini Index will rise as the vintage of accounts matures. However don't expect it to rise to the level of the overall Gini produced from the scorecard development. For a fair comparison, the development sample Gini should be recalculated based on the cut-off set, ie excluding the Rejects. The effect will be a lower target Gini.

Projecting performance

A typical scorecard performance period (excluding short term loans) is between 18 months and two years. So in terms of tracking the resultant Bad rates and comparing them with predicted results, we could wait this period of time, but if things are going wrong, we need to identify them as soon as possible. Before we get into drilling down into finding problems with a scorecard, we should look at the bigger picture: Based on the early Bad rates, can we forecast where they will be at the point of scorecard maturity?

Figure 11.3 shows one way of tracking the Bad rates by vintage from the example in Figure 11.1. Each vintage's Bad rates is growing in the fashion shown in Figure 11.4. This Bad rate over time curve, is often referred to as the Life Cycle Effect of the accounts; a natural worsening of the Bad rates as the exposure increases to maturity.

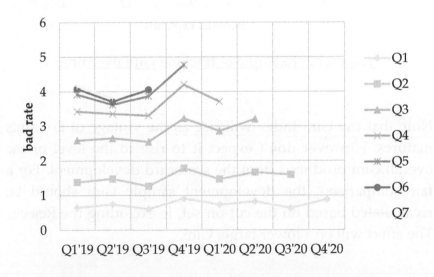

Figure 11.3: Example Vintage Analysis Graph

If the business has a standard curve, then each period's current Bad rate performance can be projected to the point where they can be compared with that of the scorecard's expected result. Let's see this in action. Using the curve in Figure 11.4, this rate of growth is applied to the observed results shown in Figure 11.1. The completed table is shown as Figure 11.5, where all vintages are projected out for 7 quarters.

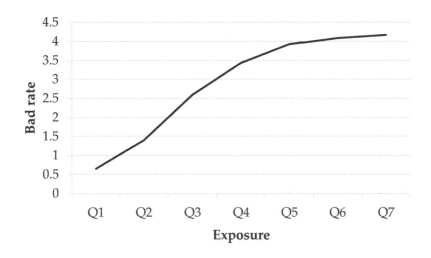

Figure 11.4: Example Bad rate maturity curve

| | | Quarter Exposure Observed | | | | | | |
		Q1	Q2	Q3	Q4	Q5	Q6	Q7
Quarter Advanced	Q1'19	0.65	1.39	2.59	3.43	3.92	4.08	4.17
	Q2'19	0.74	1.48	2.65	3.36	3.62	3.71	3.82
	Q3'19	0.61	1.27	2.55	3.31	3.87	4.06	4.14
	Q4'19	0.91	1.79	3.23	4.2	4.77	4.97	5.07
	Q1'20	0.73	1.47	2.86	3.71	4.24	4.42	4.51
	Q2'20	0.82	1.67	3.21	4.25	4.86	5.06	5.16
	Q3'20	0.63	1.60	2.98	3.95	4.51	4.70	4.79
	Q4'20	0.88	1.88	3.51	4.64	5.31	5.53	5.64

Figure 11.5: Example Vintage Analysis Report with projected performance

A SHORT STORY

A mail order firm appointed consultants to look at the portfolio reporting and profitability by score. The firm had multiple scorecards, split by type of promotion (and therefore the type of data captured) however there was no specific tracking of scorecards. The reason for this was that the Credit Department looked at overall performance, tying this back to the company's risk appetite. The scorecards were the purview of the Operational Research Department who were a smart team with a long list of models scheduled for development, both for credit risk assessment and for marketing purposes. When asked about tracking, they said that the credit scorecards could be expected to be reliable for 3 years and their schedule allowed for a rebuild at that time.

So there was no tracking of Bad rates by score and when the consultants looked at profitability by score they noticed some very poor performance for score bands, particularly .near the cut-off. Further delving, highlighted a discrepancy between the data captured and data used, allowing thin files to be approved that subsequently performed out of line with expectations. Overall the performance wasn't too bad, but without analysing the performance by score, the weakness would never have been found and may have been replicated in subsequent scorecard developments.

This approach can be taken further. The problem with Bads is they are often defined as 3 months in arrears, so it takes longer to determine the performance than may already be indicted by earlier arrears. To get around this, many companies look at projecting Bad rates from early arrears.

Let's look at an example where we have an expected Bad rate (EB) based on the recent applicant profile, but this Bad rate should take 12 months to mature. From tracking the percentage of cases in arrears by arrears level we may find that, on average, the relationship between 1+ in arrears after 3 months and Bad after 6 months is 2.5x and the relationship between Bad after 12 months and Bad after 6 months is 2x. Then we can estimate that the Bad rate after 12 months is 5x the 1+ in arrears after 3 months.

Of course there will be errors associated with such an estimation, but working backwards, using a confidence interval (see Equation 11.2) will enable the credit analyst to determine whether an observed variation at 3 months might be significant. This is illustrated in Equation 11.2, where B% is the expected Bad rate from the scorecard, F is the factorial relationship between the Bad rate after the performance period (say 12 months) and the 1+ arrears level after 3 months. N is the sample size of the vintage observed at the 3 month exposure. S refers to the standard deviation of the predicted 1+(3m) figures obtained when the factor was investigated and n the sample size .

$$\text{Expected } 1+(3m) = \frac{B\%}{F} +/- 1.96 \times \frac{S}{\sqrt{n}}$$

Equation 11.2: Creating an Expected early outcome metric

TOOL EIGHT

PROJECTING PERFORMANCE

As an example,

Bad rate = 1+(6m) x F +/- e

Where Bad rate is the outturn expected after the appropriate exposure (performance period), F is a factor being applied to the proportion of 1+ arrears cases after 6 months and e is the error.

The error is found in the modelling process, looking at the standard deviation of the results.

TIPS

PROJECTING PERFORMANCE

- Determine a Life Cycle curve of bad rates which will give the relationship (factors) between any exposure and another – but principally the scorecard performance period

- Relationships between early arrears levels are ideal for exposures of less than 6 months

- Remember this is about units and not the value since we are evaluating the scorecard rather than expected loss.

12

Scorecard Performance

What can go wrong?

David Kindred - a seasoned Chief Risk Officer - once said, "Implementing a scorecard without monitoring performance is like driving a car without checking the speedometer or fuel consumption." I couldn't agree more since there are numerous things that can go wrong. These include:

- Errors made in the initial modelling process
- Socio demographic shifts that devalue predictiveness
- Data changes, such as CRA reporting
- Product changes that impact account performance
- Marketing that attracts a variation in the population
- Competition that impacts the applicant population
- The economy

It's vital to assess the scorecard prior to deployment, using a Hold-out sample or similar test group, but also a more recent sample. However it is still possible for shifts or data errors to still creep in and in Chapter 4 we looked at analysis of the score profile to highlight any potential problems.

Of course the first real test of the scorecard is when we see performance of the accepted accounts. In Chapter 11 we looked at the overall performance and this is fine providing there is no significant variation from the predicted value. If there is however, we need to drill down and look at the performance by score. Table 12.1 illustrates a scorecard performance report showing the credit risk by score band (after a specified performance period). The Good:Bad Odds is the number of Goods divided by the number of Bads. However if we just look at this performance we might identify a scorecard as not performing when it is.

Score band	#Goods	#Bads	Interval Bad rate	Good:Bad Odds	Info Odds
1	16	14	46.7%	1.1	0.05
2	80	21	20.8%	3.8	0.17
3	177	34	16.1%	5.2	0.24
4	301	27	8.2%	11.1	0.51
5	610	18	2.9%	33.9	1.54
6	710	13	1.8%	54.6	2.49
7	678	11	1.6%	61.6	2.81
8	240	3	1.2%	80.0	3.64
9	120	1	0.8%	120.0	5.46
10	210	1	0.5%	210.0	9.56
Total	3142	143	4.4%	22.0	1.0

Table 12.1: Example Scorecard Performance report

During the 1990's recession in the UK, many bank had recently started relying on credit scores but saw a sharp rise in delinquencies and subsequent losses and blamed the scorecards. Figure 12.1 illustrates what happened to Bad rates by score between the benign period - when the development sample was taken and the recessionary period. Note that the Bad rates for the higher credit scores didn't deteriorate as much as for the lower scores.

What we looked at in Chapter 9 was the discrimination of the principal sets: Good and Bad. Our cut-off strategy depends on the absolute credit risk, either overall or at the margin, but the determination of whether a scorecard is working should be irrespective of the overall (or population) risk.

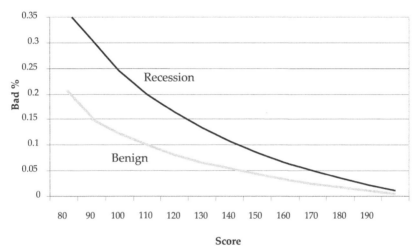

Figure 12.1: Illustration of Recessionary impact on Bad rates

That's why the report in Table 12.1 included the "Info Odds", short for Information Odds. Equation 12.1 shows the calculation of these odds for each score band "i" which thereby removes the risk of the population. Note that the total Information Odds are 1.

A SHORT STORY

A short term loan company received a vast number of applications—hundreds of thousands a month—of which around 15% were approved. The short duration of the loans mean that the performance could be evaluated within 60 days of the advance. Predictive scorecards were developed using rich data that would have taken lower volume, longer term loan companies years to interpret.

Very soon, the lender realised that the scorecards became misaligned quite quickly, and within the first year, a more complex decision system was built that included neural networks and Vector Machine models.

The rate of redevelopment and the 'black box' approach resulted in the company moving rapidly to allow the models to be adaptive—learning and recalibrating themselves.

However over the next two years, with a cut-off based on maintaining the credit risk, the acceptance rate slid from 15% to 10% and then to 8%. After 3 years the acceptance rate was heading for 6%. Machine Learning is great, but more than 85% of the applicants were rejected, with no performance to assess. This was a self-selection problem with biased data being modelled and resulting in the ever tightening of the cut-off.

$$\text{Info Odds}_i = \frac{\#\text{Goods}_i}{\#\text{Bads}_i} \times \frac{\text{Total }\#\text{Bads}}{\text{Total }\#\text{Goods}}$$

Equation 12.1: Information Odds formula

So, to determine whether the scorecard is still working, we should really look at the alignment of the observed Information Odds compared to the expected Information Odds.

Scorecard Misalignment

Let's consider Figure 12.2 where the Observed Information Odds are below the Expected. We can compare these two lines by looking at an Odds Index taking the natural log of the ratio of the two as shown in Equation 12.2, where IOO is the Information Odds Observed for a score band "i" and IOE is the Information Odds Expected for that same score band.

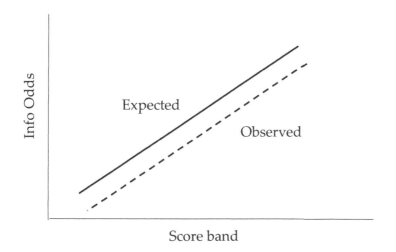

Figure 12.2: Comparing scorecard performance

121

Odds Index$_i$ = (IOO$_i$ /IOE$_i$)

Equation 12.2: Odds Index

We can repeat this for each score band and calculate an overall Misalignment Index as shown in Equation 12.3. Here we need to make the individual components positive so that they can't compensate for one another. By multiplying each Ln Odds Index by the proportion in the score band we weight their contribution so that the Index isn't skewed by a score band with low counts. The Misalignment Index is often expressed as a percentage.

Misalignment Index = Σ %Accounts$_i$ x |Ln Odds Index$_i$|

Equation 12.3: Misalignment Index

Score band	%Accounts	IOE	IOO	Ln (IOO/IOE)	MI
1	1%	0.054	0.033	-0.490	49.0%
2	3%	0.170	0.161	-0.056	5.6%
3	6%	0.244	0.188	-0.259	25.9%
4	10%	0.515	0.507	-0.015	1.5%
5	19%	1.539	1.423	-0.078	7.8%
6	22%	2.521	2.085	-0.190	19.0%
7	21%	2.695	2.417	-0.109	10.9%
8	8%	3.496	3.096	-0.122	12.2%
9	4%	5.242	4.954	-0.057	5.7%
10	6%	9.171	9.558	0.041	4.1%
Total	100%	1.000	1.000		11.8%

Table 12.2: Example Misalignment Report and calculation

Table 12.2 shows an example of this calculation with an overall Misalignment Index of almost 10%. As you'll see from the Tool summary in this section, any value greater than 10% is significant and worth investigating. It suggests that there is enough misalignment between the Observed and Expected performance to justify further analysis and suggests the scorecard is sub-optimal.

In the next chapter, we'll look at individual characteristics and an approach to handling some misalignment problems.

TOOL NINE

MISALIGNMENT INDEX

Misalignment Index =

Σ %Accounts$_i$ x |Ln Odds Index$_i$|

for each score band "i" where %Accounts are the number of accounts observed and |Ln Odds Index$_i$| is the modulus of the natural log of the Odds Index.

Odds Index =

(Info Odds Observed / Info Odds Expected)

RULE OF THUMB

MISALIGNMENT INDEX

Stability Index	Action
Less than 10%	Monitor
10% to 20%	Tune
Over 20%	Redevelop?

TIP

- Always 'eyeball' the distribution for a localised problem.

EXERCISE EIGHT

CALCULATE THE MISALIGNMENT INDEX

Calculate the MI for this scorecard and plot MI x %Accounts for each row to highlight the problem.

Score band	%Accounts	IOE	IOO	Ln (IOO/IOE)	MI
1-9	2%	0.12	0.15		
10-19	3%	0.28	0.29		
20-29	4%	0.40	0.41		
30-39	7%	0.73	0.67		
40-49	13%	1.12	1.01		
50-59	16%	1.55	1.35		
60-69	18%	2.80	2.77		
70-79	12%	5.33	5.28		
80-89	11%	6.56	6.68		
90-99	8%	16.17	15.97		
100+	6%	18.61	17.44		
Total	100%	1.000	1.000		

13

Characteristic Performance

Characteristic Analysis

In Chapter 6 we looked at the Characteristic Average Score Analysis which focused on the applicant profile before we know anything about performance. Table 13.1 shows a Characteristic Odds Report for Residential Status with observed results of proportions applying, acceptance rates and subsequent performance. These data would be for a vintage of accounts. Ideally the exposure would be equal to that of the scorecard performance period, but not necessarily. If it's not, the report still shows the progression of the Odds and the relationship between the performance and acceptance rate.

Since a higher average score should equate to a lower Bad rate, we should see the Information Odds fall as the acceptance rates fall. This is observed in Table 13.1.

Attribute	Applicant %	Acceptance	Info Odds
Owner	48%	85%	3.81
Renter	30%	25%	0.71
LWP	15%	13%	0.30
Other	7%	55%	1.92
Total	100%	54%	1.00

Table 13.1: Example Characteristic Odds Report

However, Table 13.2 shows a pattern that's less clear. Visa + MC has a slightly higher acceptance rate to MasterCard and yet has worse performance. Visa on its own has a good acceptance rate of 80% and yet the odds are below 1. This attribute in particular looks like there is a significant mismatch between the point score being assigned and the subsequent performance.

Attributes	Applicant %	Acceptance	Info Odds
None/NA	23.1%	33.4%	0.72
MasterCard	20.1%	83.2%	1.50
Visa	38.5%	80.1%	0.83
Visa + MC	18.3%	83.5%	1.28
Total	100.0%	70.6%	1.00

Table 13.2: Another example Characteristic Odds Report

Score Odds

Rather than look at the overall performance of the attributes within a characteristic, we could drill down into this performance. In Chapter 12 we looked at the misalignment report, in other words, the relationship between the score and the Information Odds. We compared the Observed result with the Odds expected from the scorecard development statistics.

If we have enough cases, then looking at the score vs the Odds by attribute, would identify whether the attribute is performing in line with expectations.

Figure 13.1 illustrates how the Information Odds might vary by score for the attribute Visa performing much worse than expected. Note that the Expected line should be the same for all attributes for all characteristics. If it isn't then the scorecard was misaligned from the outset—so check it as part of the scorecard validation.

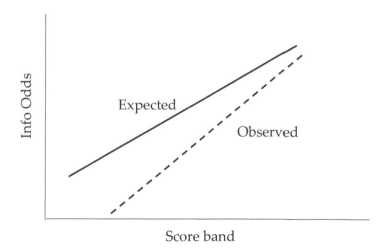

Figure 13.1: Score-Odds for the "Visa" example

Just like we did for the overall scorecard, we can calculate a Misalignment Index for each attribute. In fact we can do this for non-scorecard attributes as well, if you think there may be other variables that are now predictive. Remember that we need to compare like with like, so this time the outcome observed should be at the same exposure as for the Expected performance.

Table 13.3 shows the Misalignment Report for the Visa attribute of the Credit Cards characteristic. Note the information odds Expected (IOE) are the same as in Table 12.2. The distribution of approved accounts and the IOO are specific to this attribute. Also note that the Information odds in Table 13.2 are calculated on the basis of the proportions of Goods and Bads over the characteristic whereas within an attribute they add up to 1.

Score band	%Accounts	IOE	IOO	Ln (IOO/IOE)	MI
1	0%	0.054	-	-	-
2	1%	0.170	0.178	0.044	4.4%
3	5%	0.244	0.274	0.118	11.8%
4	8%	0.515	0.642	0.221	22.1%
5	24%	1.539	1.541	0.001	0.1%
6	28%	2.521	2.008	-0.227	22.7%
7	17%	2.695	2.010	-0.293	29.3%
8	8%	3.496	4.058	0.149	14.9%
9	4%	5.242	5.414	0.032	3.2%
10	5%	9.171	9.310	0.015	1.5%
Total	100%	1.000	1.000		15.2%

Table 13.3: Misalignment Report for "Visa" example

Spotting Misalignment Early

The Misalignment Index calculated in Table 13.3, is high, but we could see from Table 13.2 that there was a problem. However the comparison of Observed vs Expected performance means waiting as much as two years for the results. The good news is that we can look at this much earlier. Remember the section on projecting the performance in Chapter 11? We can therefore use this approach to project the Observed Information Odds at a much earlier point in the Life Cycle.

Fine Tuning a Scorecard

As we've established, just because the Bad rates aren't what were predicted, doesn't mean the scorecard is discriminating any worse than expected. We establish the latter by looking for misalignment. Of course, if a scorecard isn't performing as expected we could rebuild it, but this requires the developer to have enough data that has an adequate exposure.

The company may identify misalignment much earlier on— and then use the projected performance to identify which variables are a problem. The reaction of many companies is to address the problem with a cut-off change or subjective adjustment of the scores. However, this can be achieved more scientifically using the Odds Index that we discussed in Chapter 12.

Equation 13.1 shows the calculation of a point score using a
Weight of Evidence (WoE). In Chapter 1 we discussed how
this was the basis of early scorecard development.

$$\text{Point Score} = A \times \beta \times \text{WoE} + c$$

Equation 13.1: Weight of Evidence-based point score

In Equation 13.1, A is a factor applied to all variables
(originally done so that decimals became manageable
integers), β is the correlation coefficient, and c is a scalar that
must be applied to all attributes within a characteristic but can
vary across characteristics (originally done by Fair Isaac so
that non-credit bureau variables were always positive).

It doesn't matter that our scorecard wasn't originally a Weight
of Evidence-based one, when looking at a single characteristic,
this equation may be applied. The first thing we need to know
is A. Many scorecards are modified so that a number of points
doubles the Odds. Equation 13.2 shows such a formula, where
P is the number of points to double the odds. For example if
the developer wanted the Odds to double at every 20 points
(P), A would be 28.85 (ie 20/Ln2).

$$A = P / \text{Ln}(2)$$

Equation 13.2: Calculating a scorecard factor

Let's take the "Credit Card" characteristic, and assume we
have projected the Observed performance so that we can
calculate an Odds Index. Table 13.4 shows this calculation.

Attribute	Expected Bad rate	Observed Bad rate	EIO	OIO	Odds Index
None/NA	7.27%	8.23%	0.72	0.72	0.00
MasterCard	4.25%	4.11%	1.27	1.50	0.17
Visa	5.67%	7.18%	0.94	0.83	-0.12
Visa + MC	4.15%	4.78%	1.30	1.28	-0.02
Total	5.3%	6.0%	1.0	1.0	0.03

<u>Table 13.4: Odds Indexes for "Credit Cards" example</u>

The Odds Index effectively gives us the shift in Weights of Evidence, so we can adjust the old point score by considering this factored by A and the β, allowing for correlation. This is often referred to as the Delta score. The resultant equation is shown as Equation 13.4, below.

$$\text{New Score} = \text{Old Score} + A \times \beta \times \text{Odds Index}$$

<u>Equation 13.4: Adjusting point score using Odds Index</u>

Let's take the example in 13.4 and for this exercise, assume the scorecard factor is 28.85 and β is 1. The results are shown in Table 13.5.

So looking at the Visa attribute, the Odds Index implies a shift of 4.8 (ie 28.85 x 1 x -0.12). If we were to use all score shifts thus calculated, the average Delta would be -0.5. To ensure that the overall shift is zero, this number is then subtracted from the score shift for each attribute to give the adjusted score shift. Clearly, it's a small number in this example, but it's important to check for in case it has a material impact on the cut-off.

Attribute	Old Points	Delta score	Adj score shift	New Points
None/NA	22	-0.1	0.4	22
MasterCard	39	4.8	5.3	44
Visa	35	-3.5	-3.0	32
Visa + MC	42	-0.4	0.1	42
Average	34.5	-0.5	0.0	36.0

Table 13.5: New scores for "Credit Cards" example

In the above example we assumed the correlation coefficient was one. If the correlation coefficients are available from the scorecard development, then use the appropriate ones. If they aren't and A is known, then. β can be estimated by comparing the actual point scores with those calculated using the WoE formula in Equation 13.1.

Practical Considerations

Due to the relationships between variables, the point score fine tuning approach should be done one characteristic at a time. Best practice is to select the characteristic with attribute producing the biggest Misalignment Index. Once the new scores are calculated, the data needs to be rescored and further misalignment investigated.

134

This approach effectively assumes the misalignment is parallel, having the same impact across scores. In Table 13.3 we say an example where the Odds Index (ie the shift) varied by score band. In this case, the analyst may select a range of scores, combine them and use that Odds Index to calculate a Delta Score shift. It's most common to look for large enough cell counts and focus around the cut-off since this is where the impact will be felt.

Remember, this tuning approach is an approximation and should only be used where there is insufficient history or data to justify a full redevelopment.

TOOL TEN

INFORMATION ENTROPY and DELTA SCORES

Information Entropy (IE) = Ln |Odds Index$_i$|

for an attribute of a characteristic each score band "i" where %Accounts are the number of accounts observed and |Odds Index$_i$| is the modulus of the Odds Index (see Tool 9).

Delta Score = IE x A - b

where IE is the Information Entropy for an attribute of a characteristic, A is the scorecard multiplier (eg 28.86 for 20 points doubles the odds) and b the adjustment.

TIPS

FINE TUNING

- Use Delta Scores when a full redevelopment isn't justified or possible

- Don't forget "b" - the average shift for the characteristic - which should be adjusted to be zero

- Perform the tuning on one characteristic at a time. Due to correlation, the other characteristic's IE may change.

EXERCISE NINE

FINE TUNE THE "BANK" CHARACTERISTIC

Calculate the Information Entropy for "Bank"

Attribute	Expected Bad rate	Observed Bad rate	Expected Info Odds	Observed Info Odds	Ln (IOO/IOE)
None/NA	7.33%	0.00%	1.00	N/A	
Barclays/Lloyds	4.99%	6.13%	1.07	0.98	
NatWest/HSBC	5.06%	5.87%	1.05	1.02	
Others	6.39%	6.10%	0.82	0.98	

Then use the Delta Score approach to fine tune this characteristic. Assume a scaling factor of 100 has been used (ie A = 100)

Attribute	Proport^n	Old Point Scores	Delta Score	Adj Score shift	New Point Score
None/NA	0.0%	20			
Barclays/Lloyds	49.8%	35			
NatWest/HSBC	39.9%	34			
Others	10.3%	30			
Total / Average	100%	34.4			

14

Introduction

Behavioural scoring is almost identical to application scoring with a few exceptions:
- Sample
- Variables
- Use

The sample is of existing customers to assess existing customers. Typically, Behavioural Scoring isn't more predictive of future performance than the application score for at least 6 months. Clearly, this is because it takes time to observe the customer's behaviour. This means that samples typically exclude accounts that have been on the books for a short period. However it depends on the use, which we'll come to. The variables important for application scoring may still be predictive over the life of an account and application as well as credit bureau data should be considered, but the most predictive information is around the transactions and interactions by the customer. Many of these variables will need calculating and developers will might consider a hundred or so ratios, looking at things like time since a payment was received, the payment to amount due and over a range of periods.

Behavioural scores are used to make decisions regarding the customer's accounts, such as:

- Increasing credit limits
- Advancing further funds
- Issuing product facilities
- Approving transactions
- Collecting

When you think about the above, it becomes clear that we are using behavioural scoring to encourage the good customers and mitigate the risk or exposure to risk of the ones more likely to default.

And therein lies the problem. The whole purpose of Behavioural Scoring is to change behaviour. Think about Collections: if we didn't get more people to pay earlier, then the scorecards aren't working.

Reporting

Figure 14.1 shows an example of a Performance Report where we have the Total and number of Bads with their balances by behavioural score. Note that the accounts are being reviewed at a specific outcome period: 6 months after being scored. This could be used for calculating the Gini Index, but we are deliberately undermining the separation by our various strategies.

140

Take a look at figure 14.2. This shows a collections model with a different strategy for each of three segments.

SUMMARY PERFORMANCE REPORT

PRODUCT: BLUE CARD
SCORECARD: CREDIT LIMIT CONTROL

ACCOUNTS SCORED: JAN 2019
OUTCOME PERIOD: 6 MONTHS

SCORE	BY NUMBER			BY VALUE 000's		
	TOTAL	BADS	BAD%	TOTAL	BADS	BAD%
0	380	173	45.5%	£1,756	£719	40.9%
1-9	19,620	6,937	35.4%	£179,116	£47,294	26.4%
10-19	18,542	4,197	22.6%	£217,589	£35,041	16.1%
20-29	26,866	4,672	17.4%	£213,642	£25,444	11.9%
30-39	44,195	5,426	12.3%	£455,742	£34,906	7.7%
40-49	73,985	6,445	8.7%	£670,945	£34,804	5.2%
50-59	87,551	4,949	5.7%	£837,477	£33,005	3.9%
60-69	99,634	3,891	3.9%	£1,081,600	£21,148	2.0%
70-79	63,652	1,410	2.2%	£518,835	£5,371	1.0%
80-89	56,210	857	1.5%	£253,519	£2,078	0.8%
90-99	41,192	167	0.4%	£124,870	£430	0.3%
100+	31,525	59	0.2%	£40,250	£127	0.3%
TOTAL	563,352	39,183	7.0%	£4,595,341	£240,367	5.2%

Figure 14.1 Example Summary Performance Report

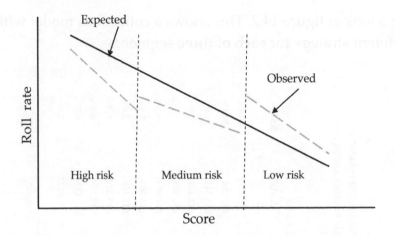

Figure 14.2 Illustration of Impact by Strategy

In Figure 14.2 we can see that the Expected and Observed performance varies by score. The very act of employing different strategies by score has yielded different results when compared with the expected. Focus on the High risk accounts has improved their expected performance but at the expense of the Low risk accounts.

The only way to know whether the scorecard performed as anticipated would be to maintain a control group for which the actions are always the same. This sounds like a good solution but is impractical. If a business knows that a new strategy out performs an old one, then it would be foolish to keep a chunk of accounts on the old strategy just for the purposes of building a scorecard and understanding the impact of strategy vs scorecard deterioration. What the company is more likely to do is run Champion/Challenger strategies to get the most out of a portfolio.

A SHORT STORY

A bank used behavioural scoring for their credit card portfolio. Four times a year they selected customers based on this score and made an offer of an unsecured personal loan. Historically the performance was within a narrow window of 3.6% and 4.1% Bad rate, but one vintage performed at almost 7%.

It was noticed that the acceptance rate for this group had been significantly (circa 15%) below the historical average. A high proportion of the loan applicants came from the first time they were offered a loan—which occurred between 2 and 3 quarters of them taking out a credit card.

Investigation showed the group in question had been underwritten for the credit card using different terms, as a test. The profile of customers was generally lower and also more likely to apply for a loan when offered.

The problem this highlights is that when a behavioural score is used for the decision about a product it should be built on that product. In this case the behavioural score was based on the credit card. The scorecard development sample should have been credit card customers who took loans. The performance should then have been based on the loan rather than the credit card.

So do we just give up, implement a behavioural scorecard and hope for the best?

Of course not!

Analysis

All of the statistical tests we've looked at for application scorecards apply, it's simply that the scorecard analyst must take care and consider that the strategy itself may be undermining the scorecard. In fact a successful scorecard will be most undermined and appear sub-optimal when it is not. When considering whether a new scorecard should be developed, the analyst should look for separation of the Goods and Bads within a strategy band, for example, Low Risk in Figure 14.2.

Characteristic Odds analysis will identify variables that are predictive and using the Odds Index it may be appropriate to fine tune a scorecard within a strategy band.

The Misalignment Index will work overall, but it is recommended that consideration be given by strategy score band.

Gini Index

Let's consider Gini, which also applies to behavioural scoring. Using the numbers from Figure 14.1, we can calculate the Gini Index for the scorecard. This is shown in Table 14.1.

Note that for this to make sense, it should be for a group of accounts after a specific exposure (like at 6 months from inception in the report shown in Figure 14.1). In this example the Gini is almost 56%. This can be compared to the Gini of the application scorecard at the point of inception (using the accepts only, so that you have a like-for-like comparison) and typically the behavioural scorecard will be more predictive from six months.

This calculation can also be done for the balances and this is shown in Table 14.2.

Score	Goods	Bads	%Gi	%Bi	CGi	Within (W)	Between (B)	Gini
0	207	173	0%	0%	0%	0.00%	0.00%	
1-9	12683	6937	2%	18%	2%	0.43%	0.00%	
10-19	14345	4197	3%	11%	5%	0.29%	0.52%	
20-29	22194	4672	4%	12%	9%	0.50%	1.23%	
30-39	38769	5426	7%	14%	17%	1.02%	2.60%	
40-49	67540	6445	13%	16%	30%	2.12%	5.52%	
50-59	82602	4949	16%	13%	45%	1.99%	7.50%	
60-69	95743	3891	18%	10%	64%	1.81%	9.02%	
70-79	62242	1410	12%	4%	76%	0.43%	4.58%	
80-89	55353	857	11%	2%	86%	0.23%	3.31%	
90-99	41025	167	8%	0%	94%	0.03%	0.73%	
100+	31466	59	6%	0%	100%	0.01%	0.28%	
Total	524169	39183				8.9%	35.3%	55.8%

Table 14.1 Gini calculation for the report in Figure 14.1

Score	Goods	Bads	%Gi	%Bi	CGi	Within (W)	Between (B)	Gini
0	1037	719	0%	0%	0%	0.00%	0.00%	
1-9	131822	47294	3%	20%	3%	0.60%	0.00%	
10-19	182548	35041	4%	15%	7%	0.61%	0.88%	
20-29	188198	25444	4%	11%	12%	0.46%	1.53%	
30-39	420836	34906	10%	15%	21%	1.40%	3.35%	
40-49	636141	34804	15%	14%	36%	2.12%	6.14%	
50-59	804472	33005	18%	14%	54%	2.54%	9.83%	
60-69	1060452	21148	24%	9%	79%	2.14%	9.55%	
70-79	513464	5371	12%	2%	90%	0.26%	3.51%	
80-89	251441	2078	6%	1%	96%	0.05%	1.56%	
90-99	124440	430	3%	0%	99%	0.01%	0.34%	
100+	40123	127	1%	0%	100%	0.00%	0.10%	
Total	4354974	240367				**10.2%**	**36.8%**	**53.0%**

Table 14.2 Gini calculation on balances from Figure 14.1

This balance-based statistic is not a true Gini since these aren't cases that can be "Flipped" to give a Null or Perfect scenario. However, it provides another metric that can tell us something about what's going on. If the average balance was the same for all Goods across the score bands. And all score bands had the same average Bad balance, then the Gini would be the same as for the units, ie around 56% in this example. The fact that the Gini using balances is lower (53% from Table 14.2), tells us that we are achieving worse discrimination because or either the lending strategy or the borrowing behaviour of the customers.

Considering the Financial Impact

Behavioural provides us with more metrics by which we can understand the quality of a portfolio: tracking the average behavioural score and the average behavioural score by balance intervals is commonplace.

The Population Stability Report is still useful for behavioural scoring but it also provides another metric: The Balance Stability Index. This is effectively the balance distribution by score and can be compared with the Expected distribution to appreciate where strategies may be working or not.

The formula for the Balance Stability Index (BSI) is shown in Equation 14.1 where BO is the balance index observed within a score band and BE is the balance index expected. The Balance Index formula is shown in Equation 14.2 for the observed population. BE is derived in the same way.

$$B.S.I. = \Sigma(BO - BE) \times Ln\ (BO/BE)$$

Equation 14.1: Balance Stability Index

$$BO = 2 \times \frac{\text{Score band average balance}}{\text{Overall average balance}}$$

Equation 14.2: Balance Index Observed

The BSI metric compares the distribution of balances in the same way that the Population Stability Index measured the stability of the applicant distribution. The larger the number, the greater the variation away from the expected distribution, which may suggest the need for a redevelopment, but also helps provide focus for where strategies are failing or could be improved upon.

Table 14.3 is an example of average balance distributions by score which is then illustrated as Figure 14.3. Since we typically want to increase balances for higher scoring customers (higher balance = higher income), then the example shows the company is doing all right for most score bands. 60 to 69 and the highest scores have achieved a lower index than expected and will need investigation. This is unlikely to be a scorecard problem, but rather the strategy deployed.

Score band	BO	BE	BO- BE	Ln(BO/BE)	BSI
10 -	0.4	0.5	-0.1	-0.223	0.022
20 -	1.3	1.5	-0.2	-0.143	0.029
30 -	2.2	2.4	-0.2	-0.087	0.017
40 -	2.6	2.4	0.2	0.080	0.016
50 -	2.4	2.2	0.2	0.087	0.017
60 -	2.6	3.1	-0.5	-0.176	0.088
70 -	3.9	3.4	0.5	0.137	0.069
80 -	2.9	2.8	0.1	0.035	0.004
90 -	1	1.2	-0.2	-0.182	0.036
					29.8%

Table 14.3: Example Balance Stability Index

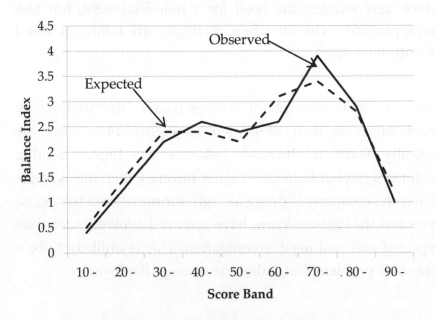

Figure 14.3: Balance Indexes Graphed

EXERCISE TEN

CALCULATE THE BALANCE STABILITY INDEX

Compare the Balance Indexes for a Champion (BE) and Challenger (BO) strategy

Score band	BO	BE	BO-BE	Ln(BO/BE)	BSI
<120	0.68	0.71			
120-149	0.83	0.91			
150-189	1.10	1.03			
190-219	1.21	1.16			
220+	1.17	1.15			

What does this tell you?

15

Scorecard Audit and Validation

Introduction

There are two stages of scorecard validation. Firstly, it should be a task performed by the scorecard developer to ensure the model and conclusions should be acceptable to the business. Secondly, it is more of an audit by the business to ensure that the scorecard was built appropriately and meets the operational needs. This applies whether the scorecard was built an in-house team or by a third party.

A vast number of assumptions and decisions are made during the modelling process, irrespective of whether the scorecard is built manually or, at the other extreme, using machine learning. It is vital that the business is comfortable with the assumptions and decisions made. The remainder of this chapter will look at these elements as well as the more obvious checks to determine if the scorecard is suitable or not.

Sample Window and Outcome Period

What period was the sample taken from? The objective is to build a model on past applications that reflects the current population. Therefore it needs to be representative. For example if the product has changed then accounts may behave differently. If application details captured have changed, were they significant? This is likely to be the case if previous decisions were influenced by those details.

Is the target population the same? If it has changed significantly, such as a shift to a younger population or financing a different product (in the retail sales sector) then the scorecard won't perform as predicted. Another example would be a major change in marketing, say from generalised promotion (eg DRTV) to direct marketing to a list such as a prospect database.

Did the developer look at seasonality of the business? In Chapter 3 we looked at Robustness—performing a statistical test to check that the predictiveness of the variable didn't change too much over the window. If the developer didn't perform this test, then the independent check should do so.

Fundamentally, accounts that are too long ago, won't represent the current population. Accounts that were too recent have a different problem. If they aren't mature enough then we will have a misclassification problem. Let's consider that issue in the next section.

There are two types of Outcome Period: firstly, the most common, where there is a single observation point at which the performance of the accounts is evaluated. This means that the exposures vary across the Sample Window. More recent applications have a shorter exposure and therefore less chance of Bads maturing. The second type is where the outcome is set the same for all vintages. In most cases, this second scenario is best so that all maturities are the same rather than requiring a view of the average maturity for monitoring purposes.

As we'll see from the next section, the setting of the Outcome Period is bound up in the determination of the Bad definition. It's worth noting that models built for Capital Adequacy purposes require a prediction of the Probability of Default (PD) after 12 months. This does not mean the Outcome Period for the scorecard should be 12 months, since for most loans, other than short-term, the point of maturity occurs between two and three years from inception. So setting a 12 month Outcome Period for the scorecard will lead to significant mis-classification of future Bads as Good accounts. The solution is to build a PD scorecard with an appropriately assessed Outcome Period and then convert this for a 12 month outcome prediction.

Bad Definition

Most lenders view a Bad to be someone with whom the company would not have done business if they had known the outcome. It may be that the company has a standard definition, say Ever 3 months in arrears, but it is best practice to evaluate the definition. The simplest way to do this is to look at roll rates. Table 15.1 shows various potential definitions of Bad at the sampling point and reviewing the subsequent outcome, in this case whether the accounts reached "write-off" - defined as 120 days past due (dpd) or worse - within 12 months.

Observation	Outcome
30 dpd	19%
Ever 30 dpd	12%
60 dpd	50%
Ever 60 dpd	29%
90 dpd	86%
Ever 90 dpd	77%
Ever 2 x 60 dpd	31%
Ever 3 x 60 dpd	29%
60 pdp and Ever 90 pdp	65%

Table 15.1: Example evaluation of a Bad definition

From Table 15.1, the developer may select Bad as any case that is 90 days past due at the Observation Point. However they will always have an eye on the number of Bads and the final choice of definition will often be a compromise between the likelihood of future write-off and the number of Bads.

Even if the company has a standard definition of say "Ever 90 dpd", it is advisable to check what this equates to in terms of future losses. This is essentially Loss Given Default (LGD) – ignoring variations in balances – which is 86% for currently "90 dpd" and 77% for "Ever 90 dpd" in the above example.

Figure 15.1 illustrates the Life Cycle curve discussed in Chapter 11 although these are different vintages viewed at the same moment, so the individual curves can't be observed. Initially, for the first ten months, the Bad rates are very low then start to rise. In this example, from 12 months the Bad rates are around 12%, rising to between 30% and 35% after two and a half years.

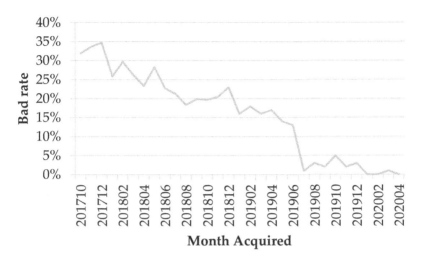

Figure 15.1: Example Bad rates for a potential sample

Clearly, any accounts selected in the first ten months will have very few Bads, but if the maturity is around 30% for all vintages, then all vintages under two years aren't fully matured.

Let's look at October 2018 (ie 201810 in the graph). The Bad rate is 20% ie a third of Bads have yet to be recognised. If all of these cases are classed as Good, then there is a clear misclassification issue.

Unless we have very large samples and maturity that doesn't take so long that we have a representation issue (ie the applications are too long ago to be representative of current applications), then the developer has to accept misclassification. As a rule of thumb, developers like to set the sample cut-off so that 80% of Bads that will arise, have arisen. So in our example the developer may be restricted to accounts booked prior to June 2018.

However, let's go back to consideration of the true Life Cycle curve. If this has been tracked and is shown that maturity occurs around two years from inception, then it could be that the snapshot shown in Figure 14.1 is misleading. The 80% maturity rule could allow the sample to include anything before early 2019.

What about sampling earlier Bads?

One method of boosting the number of Bads, without running into a misclassification issue, is to take accounts from more recent vintages that are Bad. In other words, broaden the Sample Window but exclude anything other than Bad.

If this has been done, then it should only include earlier Bads where the business believes that these Bads simply appeared earlier rather than arising due to other reasons. For example, very early Bads are likely to be Frauds and if the scorecard is to predict standard credit risk then Frauds should be excluded from the sample.

Another reason for early default may be down to underwriting issues—especially related to affordability since the customer couldn't afford repayments very early as opposed to some financial instability arising. Underwriting type issues need to be addressed separately and so shouldn't be modelled within a scorecard.

So, it's alright to include earlier Bads as long as they have been checked for reasonableness. It is unlikely that Bads arising within the first six months should be included. Of course, if the number of Bads has been boosted, then this needs to be taken into account when the strategy-curve is produced. The predicted Bad rates will need to be reduced by the appropriate amount.

Encoding

Scorecard modelling systems that are integrated into the application system have risen to the fore in recent years, especially where machine learning models are deployed. In such systems, the likelihood of error is small. However, where a model has been built by the developer writing code (SAS, R, Python, SPSS, etc) and translating variables into dummies variables or calculating further variables, there is potential for that code to be incorrect. Therefore it is always prudent to take the final scorecard and trace the variables back through the code, verifying that no errors were made in the translation.

In case you think this is unlikely, let me tell you a story: A scorecard developer working for a major consultancy built a scorecard for a client (you'll appreciate later why I can't tell you which one). He was rushed and hadn't translated his final scorecard characteristics into English. As he put together his Powerpoint presentation to management, he quickly changed the variable names into meaningful ones. However in doing this, he was horrified to find that one of his final characteristics didn't make sense. It wasn't a variable that could be in the final scorecard (for example one that isn't available at the point of decision making). Ideally he would have rebuilt the scorecard, but because he didn't have time, he simply changed the name of the characteristic to be something that was acceptable. Very fortunately for him, the company accepted the scorecard without question and goes to demonstrate why independent validation is so important.

The second component of encoding is deployment. The scorecard code should be such that the business can deploy the scorecard exactly as developed and make no further assumptions or errors.

Training vs Test

Most developers will have a Training set of data used to 'train' the model and a Test dataset against which to check the model. In traditional scoring jargon, this Test set is referred to as a Hold-out sample - because the original development database is split in two with around 20% being "held-out" as the Test dataset. This Hold-out group must be randomly sampled.

Once the scorecard has been built on the remaining, Training dataset, the test dataset is scored and the results compared with that of the development sample. As a rule of thumb, when comparing Gini Indexes, the difference should not be more than 5%. However it is not uncommon to hear the developer explain larger differences as down to the size of the sample.

QUESTIONS TO ASK:

OUTCOME DEFINITIONS

- Were Bads sampled from earlier vintages?
- Was the Bad definition reasonably tested?
- Was the Bad definition compromised to boost the numbers?
- Have frauds and suspected frauds been excluded?
- What is the Outcome Period?
- Based on expected maturity, how much mis-classification is likely?
- How does the Bad rate vary over the Sample Window?
- How was the Sample Window determined?

In my view there is no point in having a Hold-out sample if this excuse can be acceptable.

If numbers of Bads are low (say below 1,000) then the developer should question whether a Hold-out sample should be taken (with only 200 Bads). Especially since this means that the Training dataset will be left with only 800 Bads.

A better solution is to "Bootstrap" the sample to test the scorecard. In other words, build the scorecard using the full dataset and then test it against randomly selected sub-populations. In this way, multiple 20% samples can be taken, resulting in a distribution of possible outcomes.

Swap set

The Swap-set is where the benefit of the new scorecard comes from. The proportion should be calculated. It's also worth looking at the numbers of Goods and Bads in this swap, remembering that the previous rejects have had their performance inferred.

The Bad rate or Odds should be graphed for the new scorecard, showing the Known Good/Bads and the Inferred Good/Bads. The performance around the cut-off should be of particular interest. If the Bad rates of the previous rejects at scores above the cut-off are better than the Known Good/Bads, then it is likely that the Reject Inference has been overly generous. It is good practice for scorecard developers to run through Reject Inference a number of times to try and get the performance of the Rejects and the Known Good/Bads to be similar at the cut-off.

If underwriters previously overrode scorecard decisions, then a more complex, 3D Swap set is required.

It is best practice to review cases in the various Swap set cells to ensure that decisions are reasonable and Underwriting given instructions and rules on how to handle cases.

Out-of-time Sample

The next level of validation can be against a new sample of accounts. If time has moved on since the development sample was taken, more vintages will have reached the Outcome Period. If there aren't enough cases, then the analyst may increase the number of Bads by considering a more relaxed definition of Bad. For example if the scorecard was built using "Ever 3 in arrears" as the definition of Bad, then the more recent sample may be set at "Ever 2 in arrears."

Clearly, a reduced Outcome Period and / or a relaxed definition of Bad will yield lower values of the scorecard's discriminatory power. However the Out-of-time Sample is good for providing directional results. The validation process should merely consider whether the outcomes appear reasonable based on the assumptions.

Recent applications

A recent batch (usually last month's) of applications should be scored on the new scorecard to test two things: the acceptance rate and the score profile.

The acceptance rate should be in line with predictions and the profile should be compared with the expected one using the Population Stability Index. As a rule of thumb, a PSI of over 5% would warrant investigation of what had changed and whether the population may be different. A PSI of over 10% would suggest a significant change and warrant re-evaluation of the sample and potential redevelopment.

The Scorecard

The final scorecard should be reviewed for:
- Illogical point scores
- Inclusion of unavailable variables
- Inclusion of less or unreliable variables
- Binning of attributes

By illogical point scores, I mean those that can't be explained, such as a continuous variable where the progression isn't rising or falling. If there is an out-of-pattern figure then there should be a justification. This will either be something operational (such as requiring 3 years of addresses) or due to an interaction with another variable. If the latter, then this should be explored and considered as a combined variable (see Chapter 8 on interactions).

It is unusual to find a characteristic that's based on a variable that isn't available at the time of evaluation, however data capture may have changed, or the developer didn't understand the source of a field. We looked at an example in the short story in Chapter 3.

Unreliable variables should be the last considered and only included if necessary. We looked at this in Chapter 2, considering whether variables were verified or potentially influenced. Unverified income would be an example of a variable to consider unreliable as would something that may not have always been captured in the past or isn't available now.

In Chapter 2 we looked at binning variables and part of the independent audit of a scorecard should be to check how this was performed. Were attributes combined logically and based on performance – possibly using a z-test or similar? It's good practice to check the calculations as part of an independent audit.

If the variable is discrete and attributes combined, then again was it based on logic and performance? For example it may be sensible to combine Homeowners with and without a mortgage. Where there are low cell counts, especially Bads below 30, then there will be a large statistical error in the Bad rate. Relying on this to combine attributes can therefore lead to variables that appear more predictive (using an Information Value test) than is justified.

Finally, did the developer check the Robustness of the final scorecard attributes? We looked at this in Chapter three. Any attributes showing a significant variation in performance over the Sample Window

RULES OF THUMB

SCORECARD VALIDATION

The following is a guide to the acceptability of scorecard validation results

Hold out Sample Gini difference	< 5%
Population Stability Index	< 10%
Swap set	> 10%
Gini difference when Indeterminates are classed as Goods	> 5%

QUESTIONS TO ASK:

SCORECARD VALIDATION

- Was there a Hold-out or equivalent Test group used and what is the Gini?
- Was the scorecard tested on an out-of time sample, possibly relaxing the Bad definition to increase the number of Bads?
- Check Indeterminates were less than 10% of the population
- What is the impact of Indeterminates if treated as Goods?
- What is the Population Stability Index of a recent sample
- What is the Swap set and what cases have been reviewed?
- How were attributes combined?
- Were Interactions checked for?

TIPS

WHAT MIGHT BE SUSPICIOUS?

- Smoothed distributions – especially score interval Bad rates
- A large swap set
- Extreme Reject Inference
- Beneficial RI at the cut-off
- Weighting applied to the sample
- A high proportion of Indeterminates
- Spurious attribute binning
- Out of pattern (illogical) point scores
- Inclusion of problem characteristics

16

A Case Study: Sub-population

Background

An unsecured personal loan company with a loan targeted at "Affinity" groups including unions and large associations. Interest rates were excellent if not the lowest, however the applicant's tended to be "blue collar" workers and for them the interest rates were attractive. The historical 12 month Bad rate was excellent and at 1.2%, below the appetite for risk. The acceptance rate was just below 60% on average.

Looking for opportunity, the company expanded its offering to include applicants from groups that weren't signed up as "Affinity" partners. In other words there was no verification of the association. The roll out featured TV and newspaper advertising. Applications ran at around 5,000 a month, quickly matching the volume from the affinity partners.

Profile

The early indictors were good, with the acceptance rate of "Other" similar to that experienced by "Affinity". Table 16.1 is the Average Score Report (excluding the credit bureau characteristics) which shows very little movement in the average score, which was reflected in the acceptance rate of 56.6% compared with the 58.6% expected.

Characteristic	Average Scores		
	Expected	Observed	Difference
Marital Status	5.4	5.7	0.3
Age and Time at address	5.5	5.2	-0.3
Age and Accommodation	33	30.5	-2.5
Home Phone	25.9	26.2	0.3
Job Type	10.7	10.7	0
Job Status	18.5	17.9	-0.6
Time in Employment	5	3.4	-1.6
Credit Cards	10.6	11.9	1.3
Time at Bank	5.2	5.6	0.4
Loan Amount	7.5	8.7	1.2
Loan Purpose	12.5	13.1	0.6
Total	139.8	138.9	-0.9

Table 16.1: Average Score Report after roll-out

Table 16.2 shows the applicant distributions and Population Stability Index. The PSI is high, but not at the 10% trigger and the biggest variations appeared to be below the cut-off.

Outturn

The observed Bad rate after 6 months was 0.94. The Life Cycle modelled from vintage analysis (see Chapter 11) suggested that the 12 month Bad rate would be 2.55 times the 6 months Bad rate. Therefore our predicted Bad rate at 12 months is 2.4%. So it was heading to be almost double.

As we saw, the PSI was below 10% and the average scores were hardly changed, and yet the performance is very different. Let's use Chi Squared to see if there's anything going on (note that it's based on %s, so the critical value is unreliable). Table 16.3 shows the Chi Squared value for Residential Status is low. However Table 16.4 shows that for Job Status it could be significant.

Score band	Expected Distrb	Observed Distrb	0%-E%	Ln(0%/E%)	PSI
<=79	1.9%	2.3%	-0.5%	-18.2%	0.1%
80-89	2.1%	3.0%	-1.5%	-47.0%	0.7%
90-99	3.9%	4.4%	0.5%	9.5%	0.0%
100-109	5.1%	6.7%	3.5%	69.3%	2.4%
110-119	7.9%	8.6%	-3.5%	-57.5%	2.0%
120-129	12.0%	11.2%	-3.0%	-43.5%	1.3%
130-139	17.2%	14.6%	-3.3%	-34.5%	1.1%
140-149	19.3%	16.6%	0.9%	9.0%	0.1%
150-159	16.8%	15.0%	0.2%	2.3%	0.0%
160-169	9.8%	11.4%	1.7%	14.4%	0.2%
170-179	3.1%	4.9%	3.5%	23.1%	0.8%
>=180	0.9%	1.3%	1.5%	10.2%	0.2%
	100.0%	100.0%			9.0%

Table 16.2: Population Stability report after roll-out

	Expected	Observed	Chi Sq
Owner	67.3%	61.1%	0.6%
Renter	20.4%	27.4%	2.4%
Other	12.3%	11.5%	0.1%
Total	100%	100%	**3.0%**

Table 16.3: Chi Squared test for "Residential Status"

	Expected	Observed	Chi Sq
Other	9.0%	12.1%	1.1%
Clerical	68.1%	54.5%	2.7%
Manager	22.9%	33.4%	4.8%
Total	100%	100%	**8.6%**

Table 16.4: Chi Squared test for "Job Status"

We don't need to limit this test to scorecard characteristics, so let's look at the "Source" of the applications.

	Expected	Observed	Chi Sq
Affinity	86.0%	57.0%	9.8%
Other	14.0%	43.0%	60.1%
Total	100%	100%	**69.9%**

Table 16.5: Chi Squared test for "Source"

Unsurprisingly, there is a massive shift from "Affinity" to "Other". In fact when we look at the Bad rates, the biggest difference occurs for "Source". The next biggest are for "Credit Cards" and "Job Status".

The "Credit Card" characteristic is shown in Table 16.6. From this we can see that both Bad rates are higher and acceptance rates are down – which is the relationship you'd expect for a

172

downward shift in profile, but there are more people with the higher scoring attribute, "1+ cards" but the risk is over three times higher than expected.

	Expected			Observed		
	Apps	Accept rate	Bad rate	Apps	Accept rate	Bad rate
None	41%	42.4%	2.5%	34%	21.5%	5.5%
1+ cards	59%	69.8%	0.6%	66%	74.7%	1.9%
Total	100%	58.6%	1.2%	100%	56.6%	2.4%

Table 16.6: Characteristic Analysis for "Credit Cards"

Let's now look at the Odds Index for "Credit Cards". Table 16.7 shows that "1+ Cards" is significantly out of line with expectations.

	Expected Bad rate	Observed Bad rate	EIO	OIO	Odds Index
None	2.5%	5.5%	0.459	0.416	-0.10
1+ Cards	0.6%	1.9%	1.951	1.251	-0.44
Total	1.2%	2.4%			-0.54

Table 16.7: Odds Indexes for "Credit Cards"

	Old Points	Score shift	Adj score shift	New Points
None	0	-3.0	-2.5	-2.5
1+ Cards	18	0.0	0.6	17.6
Total	12.6	-0.6	0.0	12.6

Table 16.8: Fine tuning "Credit Cards"

TIPS

HOW TO IDENTIFY A SUB-POPULATION

Applicant Profile:

- The score profile shows a secondary hump
  - The profile differs for non-scoring attributes
  - The PSI of a group is significant
- Chi squared values are high despite other indicators being low.

Performance:

- The pattern of the performance by attribute differs from the main population
  - The Interaction Index are significant
  - CHAID (or similar) shows different variables entering for different branches.

Fine Tuning

If we were to take the figures in Table 16.7 and use the fine tuning approach discussed in Chapter 14 we derive the new scores in Table 16.8 if the scorecard factor was 28.85. So the net effect is a shift of only 3 points.

This suggests that the performance should be mostly addressed by a cut-off change rather than fine-tuning the scorecard... Or there's something more fundamental going on. Let's look at Source, which isn't in the scorecard, but shows very different profiles of applicants between Affinity and the Other group. In the next section we will analyse the misalignment for these two groups.

Let's also look at Source. It's not a scorecard characteristic but can be treated in the same way. Table 16.9 gives the Odds Indexes and Table 16.10 is the calculation of the effective point scores that could be added for this variable.

	Expected Bad rate	Observed Bad rate	EIO	OIO	Odds Index
Affinity	1.2%	1.6%	1.000	1.390	0.33
Other	1.2%	3.6%	1.000	0.605	-0.50
Total	1.2%	2.2%			-0.17

Table 16.9: Odds Indexes for "Source"

So we could consider adding 7.3 points to each Affinity application and deducting 16.7 from applications from other sources. Note that this doesn't address the overall risk, which is a cut-off issue, but rather the relative risk between "Affinity" and "Other".

	Old Points	Score shift	Adj score shift	New Points
Affinity	0	9.5	7.3	7.3
Other	0	-14.5	-16.7	-16.7
Total	0.0	2.2	0.0	0.0

Table 16.10: Fine tuning "Source"

Misalignment

The Misalignment reports and Misalignment Indexes have been calculated for the two groups based on "Source".

Score band	% Accepts	IOE	IOO	Ln (IOO/IOE)	MI
145-149	18.8%	0.400	0.390	-0.025	2.5%
150-154	18.9%	0.800	0.790	-0.013	1.3%
155-159	16.5%	1.440	1.470	0.021	2.1%
160-164	15.7%	1.910	2.010	0.051	5.1%
165-169	15.2%	2.650	2.550	-0.038	3.8%
170-174	8.1%	4.050	3.940	-0.028	2.8%
175-179	3.1%	6.200	5.930	-0.045	4.5%
180+	3.7%	8.980	9.540	0.060	6.0%
Total	100%	1.000	1.000		3.0%

Table 16.11: Misalignment Report for "Affinity"

Table 16.11 is the report for "Affinity" and yields a Misalignment Index of 3%. So this performance is in-line with expectations. Table 16.12 repeats this for "Other" and tells us that this scorecard has a major problem and is significantly out of line with the development expected performance by score.

Score band	% Accepts	IOE	IOO	Ln (IOO/IOE)	MI
145-149	18.9%	0.400	0.600	0.405	40.5%
150-154	18.0%	0.800	0.700	-0.134	13.4%
155-159	15.2%	1.440	0.600	-0.875	87.5%
160-164	14.6%	1.910	2.430	0.241	24.1%
165-169	13.5%	2.650	2.410	-0.095	9.5%
170-174	9.9%	4.050	3.160	-0.248	24.8%
175-179	6.2%	6.200	3.000	-0.726	72.6%
180+	3.7%	8.980	7.490	-0.181	18.1%
Total	100%	1.000	1.000		35.8%

Table 16.12: Misalignment Report for "Other"

From these we can see that the problem doesn't lie with the "Affinity" performance by score, but rather the suitability of the scorecard for "Other" applications. Such a high Misalignment Index suggests the scorecard should be redeveloped for this group.

Interaction

Looking purely at the non-credit bureau data, the CHAID analysis in Figure 16.1 shows how the first split is by Age of applicant, but after that the source ("Affinity" vs "Other") matters which then results in either Residential Status or Credit Cards as being the most significant split when performing a Chi Squared test.

Let's use the Interaction Index discussed in Chapter 8, to identify whether there is potential interaction going on between Source and Credit Cards and another checking between Source and "Job Status. Table 16.13 shows the former for which the Interaction Index is 0.63.

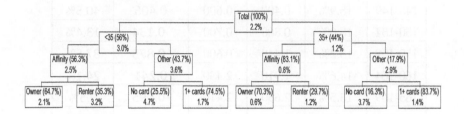

Figure 16.1: Partial CHAID tree showing variation in pattern

Table 16.14 shows the Odds table for the comparison with Job Status and results in an Interaction Index of 0.91. So both metrics are significant, backing up what we saw in the CHAID analysis.

Odds	Affinity	Other	Prop^n
No Card	0.85	0.26	19%
1+ Cards	1.53	0.88	81%
Proportion	68%	32%	100%

Table 16.13: Interaction between "Source" and "Credit Cards"

Odds	Affinity	Other	Prop^n
Other	1.3	0.4	77%
Manager	1.73	1.32	23%
Proportion	66%	32%	100%

Table 16.14: Interaction between "Source" and "Job Status"

Final Scorecards

In addition to credit bureau data (variables not shown here), the scorecard rebuild resulted in two scorecards since the predictiveness of the data varied depending on whether the application came from an approved affinity relationship or not. Below are the application form variables of each scorecard with the most predictive at the top and then by descending contribution to the final separation of Goods and Bads.

"Affinity" scorecard	"Other" scorecard
Age	Age
Residential Status	Credit cards
Loan Amount	Residential Status
Employment	Time with Bank
Time in Job	Time at Address
Credit Cards	Job Status

Table 16.8: Revised scorecard characteristics

The Employment variable related to the industry sector whereas Job Status essentially provided a separation of the "blue collar" workers from "white collar". For the "Affinity

179

relationships, it appeared that the relationship with the partner outweighed the job status of the individual. This was not true for the general population. Time in Job also seems to reinforce the view that the applicant's relationship with the affinity (and time thereof) is an important consideration.

ANSWERS TO EXERCISES

EXERCISE ONE

TEST WHETHER ATTRIBUTES SHOULD BE COMBINED

Perform the z-test for differences in proportions with a Null Hypothesis of zero difference (at 95% confidence the z-test should be <= 1.96)

Attribute	n_i	b_i
6 months (n_1 and b_1)	2113	13.35%
1 year (n_2 and b_2)	1120	15.09%

$$b_a = (2113 \times 0.1335 + 1120 \times 0.159)/(2113 + 1120) = 13.95\%$$

$$b_2 - b_1 = 1.74\%$$

$$1/n_1 + 1/n_2 = 0.1366\%$$

$$z = 1.74\% / 13.95\% \times (100\% - 13.95\%) \times \sqrt{(0.1366\%)}$$

$$= 1.36\%$$

So we accept the null hypothesis and combine 6 months and 1 year.

Note that even if the z-test result was greater than 1.96, always consider the justification for an out-of-pattern performance. Is there a reasonable explanation for why 6 months could be lower risk than 1 year (ie and typically get more points)?

EXERCISE TWO

CALCULATE THE ROBUSTNESS

The "2+ dependents" attribute had the following Bads rates over time:

Period	Goods	Bads	Bad rate
Q1	381	98	20.5%
Q2	122	22	15.3%
Q3	351	31	8.1%
Q4	465	47	9.2%
Q5	641	53	7.6%
Q6	851	61	6.7%
Q7	1044	30	2.8%
Total	3855	342	8.1%

Taking the proportions of Goods and Bads for each of the Periods and populating the Information Value calculation table yields an Information Value of over 0.2. So Period within this attribute is predictive and would be a concern.

Looking at the distribution of Bad rates there are two particular outliers. Q1 has a much higher than average Bad rate and Q7 is significantly lower.

It would be worth checking whether Q7 generally has enough exposure to provide reasonable outcomes without significant mis-classification. It would also be worth finding out about Q1 and whether policy rules or underwriting changed after this to improve performance.

Looking at the Robustness, excluding Q1 and Q7 yields an IV of 0.17, which is still high. Removing Q6, yields a much lower value:

Period	%Good	%Bad	%G-%B	WoE	IV
Q2	13%	22%	-9%	-0.5256	0.047
Q3	37%	31%	6%	0.18822	0.012
Q4	50%	47%	3%	0.05331	0.001
Q5	68%	53%	15%	0.25416	0.039
Total	100%	100%			0.052

If the Sample Window can be changed to be Q2 – Q5 then this attribute can be considered, otherwise it might be reasonable to group it with another attribute or split it to be "2 dependents" vs "3+". Failing that, the variable shouldn't be used.

EXERCISE THREE

LOOK AT THE PROFILE SHIFT

Score band	Expected Distrib^n	Observed Distrib^n	O%-E%	Ln(0%/E%)	PSI
< 173	3.0%	2.5%	-0.5%	-18.2%	0.1%
173 - 181	4.0%	2.5%	-1.5%	-47.0%	0.7%
182 - 189	5.0%	5.5%	0.5%	9.5%	0.0%
190 - 197	3.5%	7.0%	3.5%	69.3%	2.4%
198 - 205	8.0%	7.5%	-0.5%	-6.5%	0.0%
206 - 213	8.5%	2.5%	-6.0%	-122.4%	7.3%
214 - 221	11.3%	8.0%	-3.3%	-34.5%	1.1%
222 - 229	9.6%	10.5%	0.9%	9.0%	0.1%
230 - 237	8.6%	8.8%	0.2%	2.3%	0.0%
238 - 245	11.0%	12.7%	1.7%	14.4%	0.2%
246 - 258	13.5%	17.0%	3.5%	23.1%	0.8%
259 +	14.0%	15.5%	1.5%	10.2%	0.2%
	100.0%	100.0%			13.1%

Tracking average score would indicate an improved profile, but the PSI would be interpreted as a "slight shift". However this is a "Cross-Over" type shift and the drop for score band 206 – 213 is most concerning no matter what the cut-off. If the cut-off is 214 or higher, the analyst should look into whether scores are incorrect or being influenced (for example by underwriters) so that a higher proportion gets approved.

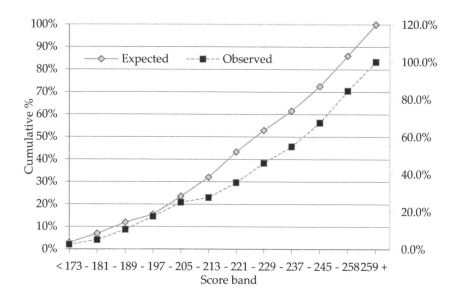

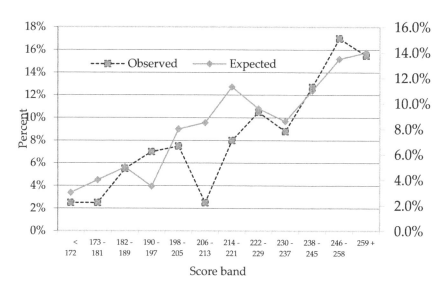

EXERCISE FOUR

AVERAGE SCORE DIFFERENCE

Attributes	Expected	Observed	Difference	Points	Shift
Owner	70.3%	88.3%	18.0%	52	9.36
Renter	13.0%	4.0%	-9.0%	43	-3.87
LWP	10.3%	1.6%	-8.7%	40	-3.48
Other	6.4%	6.1%	-0.3%	45	-0.14
Total	100.0%	100.0%			1.88

Overall, the Average Score Difference is under 2 points for the Residential Status characteristic. However there is a significant shift towards home owners and away from Renters and LWP which may be undermining the value of this characteristic.

EXERCISE FIVE

SET THE CUT-OFF

Target Acceptance Rate

To achieve 68% acceptance, the recommended cut-off would be 198.

Target Overall Bad Rate

To achieve 4.4% overall Bad rate, the recommended cut-off would be 190.

Marginal Risk

If the company needs the score interval Odds to be 11 or better, this equals a Bad rate of 8.33%. So the marginal Bad rate should be lower than 8.33%. ie the cut-off needs to be 198 or higher if a profit is to be made per account.

Note that 8.2% is the average Bad rate for the score band 198-205. If more granular Bad rates are available, then these should be used, probably yielding a cut-off of around 201.

EXERCISE SIX

CALCUALTE THE GINI

%Gi	%Bi	CGi	Within	Between
0%	1%	0%	0.00%	0.00%
1%	2%	1%	0.02%	0.00%
2%	2%	3%	0.04%	0.04%
2%	3%	5%	0.06%	0.18%
2%	4%	7%	0.08%	0.40%
2%	5%	9%	0.10%	0.70%
2%	6%	11%	0.12%	1.08%
2%	6%	13%	0.12%	1.32%
3%	8%	16%	0.24%	2.08%
3%	8%	19%	0.24%	2.56%
3%	10%	22%	0.30%	3.80%
3%	11%	25%	0.33%	4.84%
4%	10%	29%	0.40%	5.00%
4%	8%	33%	0.32%	4.64%
5%	5%	38%	0.25%	3.30%
8%	2%	46%	0.16%	1.52%
10%	2%	56%	0.20%	1.84%
11%	2%	67%	0.22%	2.24%
9%	2%	76%	0.18%	2.68%
10%	2%	86%	0.20%	3.04%
14%	1%	100%	0.14%	1.72%
		Total	**3.7%**	**43.0%**

Gini = 100% - (3.7% + 43.0%) = 53.3%

190

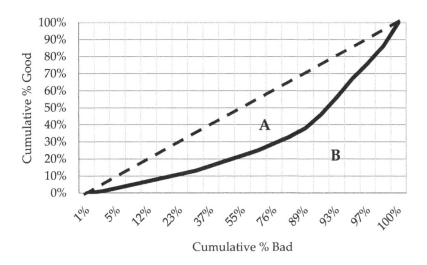

Gini Index = Area A / Area A + B

EXERCISE SEVEN

CALCUALTE THE SWAP-SET

Old Scorecard	Old decision	New scorecard	%	Decision
Fail	Reject	Fail	10%	Reject
Pass	Reject	Fail	7%	Reject
Fail	Accept	Fail	1%	Accept?
Pass	Accept	Fail	4%	Reject
Fail	Reject	Pass	8%	Accept
Pass	Reject	Pass	5%	Reject?
Fail	Accept	Pass	5%	Accept
Pass	Accept	Pass	60%	Accept

The full Swap-Set comprises: P-R-F, R-A-F, F-R-P, and F-A-P

= 24%.

However, an appreciation of what the underwriters will do is essential. Without a policy change, a likely scenario is that F-A-F will continue to be overridden to Accept and P-R-P will continue to be overridden to Reject.

If this is the case, the new rejection rate will be 26%.

EXERCISE EIGHT

CALCULATE THE MISALIGNMENT INDEX

The overall MI for this scorecard is under 6%, so in theory not a concern, however plotting each row's %Accounts x Ln (IOO/IOE) shows a more localised problem.

.

Score band	%Accounts	IOE	IOO	Ln (IOO/IOE)	MI
1-9	2%	0.12	0.15	0.223	22.3%
10-19	3%	0.28	0.29	0.035	3.5%
20-29	4%	0.40	0.41	0.025	2.5%
30-39	7%	0.73	0.67	-0.086	8.6%
40-49	13%	1.12	1.01	-0.103	10.3%
50-59	16%	1.55	1.35	-0.138	13.8%
60-69	18%	2.80	2.77	-0.011	1.1%
70-79	12%	5.33	5.28	-0.009	0.9%
80-89	11%	6.56	6.68	0.018	1.8%
90-99	8%	16.17	15.97	-0.012	1.2%
100+	6%	18.61	17.44	-0.065	6.5%
Total	100%	1.000	1.000		5.9%

The largest misalignment of the scorecard occurs between scores 40 and 59. Almost 30% of the accounts fall between these scores.

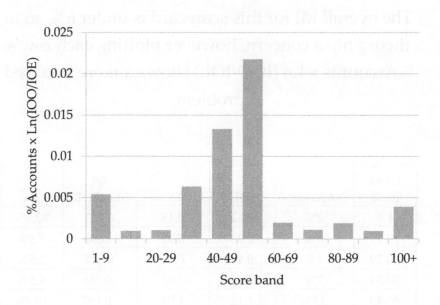

Score band

Components of MI highlighting a local issue

EXERCISE NINE

FINE TUNE THE "BANK" CHARACTERISTIC

Calculate the Information Entropy for each row of the characteristic*

Attribute	Expected Bad rate	Observed Bad rate	Expected Info Odds	Observed Info Odds	Ln(IOO/IOE)
None/NA	7.33%	0.00%	1.00	NA	NA
Barclays/Lloyds	4.99%	6.13%	1.07	0.98	-0.086
NatWest/HSBC	5.06%	5.87%	1.05	1.02	-0.026
Others	6.39%	6.10%	0.82	0.98	0.181

Then use the Delta Score approach to fine tune this characteristic, where Delta Score = IE x A - b

Here A was 100 and b can be calculated as -3.05 using the Delta scores weighted by the proportion.

Attribute	Proport^n	Old Point Scores	Delta Score	Adj Score shift	New Point Score
Barclays/Lloyds	49.8%	35	-8.2	-5.2	30
NatWest/HSBC	39.9%	34	-2.1	0.9	35
Others	10.3%	30	18.5	21.6	52
Total / Average	100%	34.4	-3.05	0.00	34.09

*Note that the attribute "None/NA" can be ignored since no applications were approved, possibly due to a policy rule.

EXERCISE TEN

CALCULATE THE BALANCE STABILITY INDEX

Score band	BO	BE	BO-BE	Ln(BO/BE)	BSI
<120	0.68	0.71	-0.03	-0.0432	0.001
120-149	0.83	0.91	-0.08	-0.0920	0.007
150-189	1.10	1.03	0.07	0.0658	0.005
190-219	1.21	1.16	0.05	0.0422	0.002
220+	1.17	1.15	0.02	0.0172	0.000
					1.6%

Despite the differences in Balance Indexes between the score bands for the Champion vs the Challenger strategy, the Balance Stability Index (BSI) is very low. This suggests that there is no indication that the Challenger strategy will perform significantly differently to the Champion.

GLOSSARY OF TERMS

Acceptance rate - The percentage of applications which are approved. See Acquisition rate.

Accepts - Applications which are accepted.

Acquisition rate - The percentage of applications which are approved and which take up the offer of credit.

Adaptability - The fit of a scorecard to a different population (see Calibration).

AI - Abbreviation for Artificial Intelligence.

Algorithm - Any computation or method involving a series of steps. The precise instructions for solving a problem.

Alignment - The adjustment of the constant and range of a scorecard to achieve a targeted risk at a specific score or value. E.g. the Odds double for every 20 points.

Application Data - The information provided by the applicant on the application form. Sometimes used to include all data at the point of application.

Application Score - Mainly, the credit score calculated on the application data alone, but also used more generally in place of credit score.

Application Processing System - A computer system or software used for processing credit applications. This may comprise the scorecard engine and strategies, workflow and rules.

Artificial Intelligence - The ability of a computer that performs operations normally associated with human intelligence.

Ascending Cumulative Statistics - A score distribution showing the percentage of applicants which can be expected to attain that score or less (see Descending Cumulative).

Attributes - A set or range of values that a characteristic can attain.

Bad Rate - The percentage of accounts which are classed as bad (see Odds and Probability of payment).

Bads - Accounts that the lender classes as those, that given hindsight, he would not have accepted.

Behavioural Scoring - A scoring system for assessing the performance of an existing account. Scores are typically risk-based but can be applied to any performance objective. Also known as Behaviour Scoring and Performance Scoring.

Big Data - Extremely large data sets that may be analysed computationally to reveal patterns.

Binning - Grouping a number of more or less continuous values into a smaller number (see Fine and Coarse classing)

Bivariate Analysis - Any form of analysis in which only two variables are considered.

Calibration - The tuning of a scorecard to fit a different or shifted population. The term is most commonly used when applied to generic or bureau scores.

CAIS - "Credit Account Information Sharing" The UK proprietary loan payment history system provided by Experian.

CCJ's - Abbreviation for County Court Judgments. A UK term whose equivalent elsewhere is Judgments, or in Scotland is Decree.

Challenger - A strategy employed as a test to be evaluated against the Champion.

Champion - A strategy employed for the majority of accounts.

Characteristic - Any variable that could appear in a scorecard. Characteristics are made up of Attributes.

Characteristic Analysis - A report on the percentage of applications (Accepts/Rejects/Goods/Bads) for each attribute of a characteristic. Monitoring reports may also include Points differences.

Chi-Squared - The statistical test of goodness of fit. Most commonly used in Credit Scoring in place of Stability Index and Information Value.

Classification Point - The point in time at which an account is observed and classified as Good or Bad. Also known as the Observation Point or the Sampling Point.

Coarse Classing - The grouping of attributes into larger groups for statistical significance. Also known as Grouping.

Cohort - A tranche of business, the delinquency of which is tracked over time.

Cohort Analysis - An alternative term for Dynamic Delinquency.

Concordance - A measure of scorecard power. It the percentage of times that the scorecard scores a good account higher than a bad account.

Continuous Characteristic - A characteristic whose range of possible values is numeric and infinite (or very large).

Control Group - The group of accounts against which no tests are applied when evaluating an alternative process, strategy or technique.

Correlation - The interdependence between two or more characteristics which can be explained by a linear relationship.

Credit Bureau - An organisation which collects and supplies credit-related information. Also referred to as a Credit Reference Agency.

Credit Bureau Score - A generic score provided by a Credit Reference Agency.

Credit Reference - The process of and information arising from an enquiry at a credit bureau.

Credit Scoring - The term for using a linear predictive model for assessing and ranking customers or applicants for credit. Also used more generally to include all types of predictive credit models.

Cross Counts - The tabulation of any characteristic against score-bands to show the score distributions of the attributes. Also the tabulation of any characteristic against another characteristic.

Cross Tabulations - An alternative term for Cross Counts. Often abbreviated to cross tabs.

Customer Relationship Management - The management of customers based on an holistic view of profitability rather than risk. Also termed Customer Value Management.

Customer Scoring - The general term for assessing and ranking customers at the customer rather than the account or product level.

Cut-off - The score below which applications are either automatically rejected or recommended for rejection.

Cut-off Strategy - The determination of the cut-off score.

Data Specification - Description of all the data considered when developing a scorecard.

Decision Trees - The organisation of information as a non-recursive partitioning of characteristics available, creating a connected graph with nodes branching into other nodes.

Declines - Applicants not granted the credit applied for.

Decree - The Scottish equivalent of the County Court Judgment in England.

Dependence - The overlap in the information contributed by two or more characteristics.

Descending Cumulative Statistics - A table of scores showing, for each score, the percentage of applicants that can be expected to achieve that score or higher.

Detailed Analysis - Alternative term for Fine Classing.

Development Sample - The group of accounts which is used to develop the scorecard.

Discrete Characteristic - A characteristic, such as residential status, where there is a finite number of potential variables.

Discriminant Analysis - A multivariate analysis classification technique similar to Linear Regression.

Distribution - The spread of occurrences.

Divergence - A measure of the separation of two distributions and used to measure the power of a scorecard.

Dynamic Delinquency - The delinquency of a cohort of business over time, showing percentages of arrears at each period of observation.

Exclusions - Accounts excluded from a scorecard development sample.

Expert System - Computer software based on expert knowledge rather than data or statistics.

Exposure Period - The length of time an account has been on the books or the time between measurement and outcome.

Final Score - The credit score which includes application data and all other, internal or external data.

Final Score Report - A report on applications during a period, showing proportions and accept rates by score.

Fine Classing - The process of defining all the possible attributes for every characteristic, and analysing each to show their Good/Bad distributions. Also known as Detailed Analysis.

Forced Accepts - Applications accepted below the cut-off. More commonly called Lowside Overrides.

Forced Rejects - Applications rejected above the cut-off. More commonly called Highside Overrides.

Generated Characteristic - A characteristic created from two or more others.

Generic Scorecard - A scorecard which has been generated when there is insufficient data to build a bespoke scorecard. Sometimes referred to as a Start-up Scorecard.

Gini Coefficient - A rank order measure of the power of a scorecard and individual characteristics that is independent of score and scale.

Good/Bad Definition - The definitions of good and bad accounts used during a scorecard development.

Goods - Accounts which a credit grantor, with hindsight would lend to again.

Gradient Boosting - A Machine Learning methodology building models in a step-wise process using optimising an arbitrary loss function.

Grey Zone - A scoreband between two cut-offs where the applications are referred to an underwriter for further investigation.

Grouping - The amalgamation of attributes into larger groups to reduce the total number of attributes and to ensure that the sample count for each one is statistically significant. Also known as Coarse Classing.

Hold-out Sample - Part of the development sample that is kept aside for validation.

Inactives - Credit or charge card accounts which are not active.

Indeterminates - Accounts for which Outcome classification cannot be determined. A term sometimes used in place of Intermediate.

Information Entropy - The degree to which the odds have drifted from the expected to the observed.

Information Odds - The ratio of the proportion of all Goods to the proportion of all Bads for an attribute or group. Contrast with Overall Odds.

Information Value - A measure of the power of a characteristic using Weights of Evidence.

Interaction - A statistical term for where the Bad rate of the combination of variables is not explained by the linear contribution of the variables.

Interaction Index - A measure of the degree of interaction expressed as the ratio of the Odds of pairs of attributes.

Intermediates - A specific term for the accounts which can be classified as neither Good nor Bad. Sometimes called Greys or Indeterminates.

Interval Odds - The Odds applying across a score band or score interval.

Interval Statistics - A table that shows the percentage of applicants by score.

Insight - The UK proprietary loan payment history system provided by Equifax.

Judgement - A formal decision handed down by a court of law. In respect of a debtor, an order to pay the creditor and the means by which this is to be achieved will also be given.

Knowledge-Based Systems - A system based on expert knowledge and inference procedures.

Kolmogorov-Smirnoff (KS) - The statistical test of a scorecards separation of its Principal Sets. Also known as Spread and Maximum Separation.

Linear Regression - A linear multivariate analysis tool for identifying correlations. Also known as OLS.

Logistic Regression - A logistic form of regression analysis in which predictors are constrained to be within the range 0 to 1.

Machine Learning – A specific sub-set of AI that trains statistical models without explicit instructions.

Marginal Odds - The Interval Odds at the scoreband just above the cut-off.

Maximum Separation - The maximum cumulative percentage difference between the Principle Sets. Alternative term for the Kolmogorov-Smirnoff statistic.

Misalignment - The situation where attributes of the scorecard are inaccurately predicting the risk.

206

Misalignment Index - A measure of the degree of Misalignment.

Multiple Linear Regression - See Linear Regression.

Neural Network - A system or modelling approach that is said to mimic the cells in the brain. The most commonly used are multi-layered with an input, output and hidden layer where each layer is a node or processing function.

Non-responders - Those people who do not respond to direct marketing.

Observation Period - The time between the application, or sampling point and the Observation Point.

Observation Point - The point in time at which an account is observed and classified as Good or Bad. Also known as the Classification Point, or the Sampling Point.

Odds - The ratio of Goods to Bads, providing a measure of risk for analysing the performance of Attributes.

Operational Grouping - Alternative term for Coarse Classing or Grouping.

Overall Odds - The product of the Population Odds and the Information Odds.

Overrides - Applications where the scorecard decision has been reversed.

Override Analysis - A report of the overrides by score bands.

Performance Scoring - Alternative term for Behavioural Scoring.

Point Scoring - Archaic term for Credit Scoring.

Points - The values assigned to each attribute of a scorecard.

Policy Rule - Any rule which is applied in addition to the scorecard.

Population - All applicants who have applied for a particular credit product.

Population Flow - A flow chart showing the breakdown of applications by performance. Often used to demonstrate sampling or performance inference.

Population Odds - A measure of the credit risk of a population. See Overall Odds.

Population Stability - A measure of the degree of similarity between the current and expected populations.

Portfolio - All accounts held by a credit grantor, typically split by product.

Pre-screening - The process of removing from a mailing list any entries which do not meet a predefined set of criteria.

Pre-screen Scorecard - A scorecard used to select prospects for mailing.

Principle Sets - The groups analysed in the scorecard, such as Good and Bad or Accept and Reject.

Profit Scoring - The statistical modelling of profit as the outcome or combination of models to comprise an aggregate profit score.

Pull List - A list of account numbers to be used in physically collecting the application data for a scorecard development.

R Squared - The statistical output of regression analysis showing the degree of correlation between score and Outcome and hence the predictiveness of a scorecard.

Random Forests – A group of models (such as Logistic Regression) constructed by using decision trees, outputting the class that is the mode or mean prediction.

Raw Score - The Weight of Evidence of an Attribute. Used less commonly to mean the score prior to alignment.

Reject Inference - The process of determining the likely performance of the rejects had they been accepted.

Rejects - Applications for credit which are not approved for credit.

Responders - People who respond to marketing.

Response Rates - The percentage of responses.

Response Scoring - The ranking of mailing prospects by propensity to respond.

Roll Rate Analysis - A report showing the proportion of accounts which move from one level of arrears to another.

Sample - The accounts selected to develop a scorecard. Also known as Development Sample.

Sampling Window - The time period from which the Development Sample is extracted. Also known as Sample Time Frame.

Sampling Plan - The plan for selecting representative examples of Good, Bad and rejected applications for scorecard development.

Sampling Point - Alternative term for Observation Point.

Score - The total number of points achieved by a prospect, applicant or customer on a scorecard.

Score Band - A narrow range of scores which are grouped together to form a statistically meaningful unit. Also known as Score Interval.

Scorecard - The general term for a ranking mechanism, typically using point scores, to predict an Outcome.

Scorecard Power - General term for the measures of a scorecard's strength. These may include R-squared, information value, coefficient of determination, Gini coefficient, divergence or Kolmogorov-Smirnoff statistic.

Solicitation Scoring - Alternative term for response scoring.

Spread - Alternative term for Maximum Separation.

Start-up Scorecard - A generic scorecard applied to a launch scenario.

Sub-population - Any sub-group within the main population which appears to be different from the rest of the population, either in terms of the data used for the credit decision or because a separate scorecard is required.

Super Fail - Applications which fail the first stage of a two stage scorecard.

Super Pass - Applications which are accepted at the first stage of a two stage scorecard.

Summary Counts - An analysis of the Development Sample by category and date.

Swap Set - Specifically, the previous accepts that are rejected and the previous rejects that are accepted under a new scoring system. More generally used for the cross count of all of the current system decisions against the new scoring system.

Total Odds - Alternative term for Overall Odds or Population Odds.

Tracking - The monitoring of a scorecard. Also known as Monitoring.

TTD - Abbreviation for Through-the Door Population. Also known as Population.

Validation - The process of testing the final scorecard before delivery.

Validation Sample - Part of the development (Hold-out) sample that is kept aside for validation. May also include a more recent sample of accounts to test the robustness due to changes in the population.

Weightings - Alternative term for Points and originated from the use of Weights of Evidence to build a scorecard.

Weight of Evidence - The predictiveness of an attribute measured as the Logarithm of the Information Odds. Also known as Raw Score.

Z-score - A commercial lending score based mainly on ratios from financial accounts.

A

Affordability · 3
American Investment Corporation · 2
Application data · 209
Artificial Intelligence · 217
AUC · 85
Average Score Difference · 52
Average Score Report · 51, 170

B

Bad definition · 155
Balance Stability Index · 148
Bhavioural Scorecard · 144, 145
Behavioural Scoring · 139, 140, 143, 148
Big Data · 217
Binning · 164
Binomial Approximation · 108
Bootstrap · 162

C

C5.0 · 78
Capital Adequacy · 69, 70, 155
CHAID · 77, 78, 79, 174, 177, 178
Characteristic Average Scores · 127
Characteristic Odds Report · 55, 127, 144

Characteristics · 1, 3, 7, 9, 11, 12, 16, 21, 28, 29, 44, 45, 48, 51, 52, 53, 54, 80, 123, 129, 132, 159, 168, 170, 172, 179, 200, 202, 204
Chi Squared · 21, 22, 23, 25, 29, 34, 77, 171, 172, 177
Confidence Interval · 108
Confusion Matrix · 89, 90, 95
Credit Bureau Score · 38, 63
Credit Scoring: The Principles and Practicalities · 103

D

Data Cleansing · 16
Delta Score · 133 - 135, 136, 138, 195
Divergence · 33, 83, 84
Durand, D · 1

E

EAD · 70
Expected Loss · 69
Expert Model · 63

F

FaceBook · 219
Fair Isaac · 1, 4, 23, 73, 75, 132
Fair, B · 2

215

You may also like

CREDIT SCORING PRINCIPLES AND PRACTICALITIES

Edited by Murray L Bailey

Chapters:

Article: Big Data, Little Data and Data Science

Big Data

Artificial Intelligence - what in the scoring-world we used to call "New Technology" - has been around for decades but made little impact on credit scoring until the late 2000s. The change was precipitated by the explosion of so-called Big Data, open-source and cloud computing. The amount of data produced grows exponentially, with a predicted 150 billion networked sensors by the end of this decade although such predictions are becoming harder to make as satellite systems are rapidly being developed to provide a global wireless internet service, increasing access and speeds.

Back in 2006 I designed the application system for a new pay-day lender. The pilot launch (under another brand name) resulted in a staggering one hundred thousand applications within a three month trial. From this huge dataset we were able to build initial models since the outcome from the loan was typically less than 45 days. We built a traditional logistic regression scorecard but within a wide Grey Zone used a neural network and a KVM model. I'd wanted a Nearest Neighbor solution but we didn't have the computing power within the production environment to support it. The three models provided the 'bidding system' that I'd envisaged and it worked exceptionally well.

With the aid of a data science team, after a number of iterations, we let the system update itself - although there was a tendency for it lead to a lower acceptance rate if reject inference wasn't considered. This is the classic issue of AI. A model built on biased data will result in an exacerbation of those biases. It will furthermore favour characteristics influenced by that bias in its decision making.

The other area to be aware of was the grouping and interpretation of new data. As well as thousands of pieces of data from the credit bureau (both provided and calculated), LenderA accessed social media data and also used interactive information captured during the application. In the good old days of paper application forms, fraudulent applications could be spotted by "floating points". These were dots on the form where the fraudster had rested their pen as they perhaps checked details and completed the form carefully.

I was fascinated to find that positioning of the mouse on a screen was similarly predictive of performance. Other powerful new variables included the movement of the sliders for the amount and period applied for, and the time spent on each section.

From this experience, there is no doubt that Big Data can provide a wealth of predictive information, whether the source be an employer (for salary finance), student body (for student loans) or generally the Internet, social media in particular.

However the mistake I have seen is to assume that this Big Data will be predictive. Most organisations don't have the luxury afforded to large pay-day lenders—they don't know the outcomes that would be associated with these new variables.

To obtain benefit from increased discrimination, we see either an improvement in risk or acceptance. Most organisations that I've discussed Big Data with, see the opportunity to increase acceptance—to approve people that are viewed as having "thin files" or being wrongly penalized by old credit records. The problem with this is that there is no outcome data to support the hypothesis. As a result, many companies have built 'expert models' or applied models built on other outcomes.

Data Science

AI has spawned a whole new breed of scorecard developers (if you are one, I hope you don't mind the classification), understanding the mathematics behind the algorithms, understanding the statistics but more importantly understanding the failings.

However, time and time again I come across statisticians calling themselves a Data Scientist with neither the background in AI, nor the experience as a traditional scorecard developer. Such amateurs can damage a business if allowed to build and deploy inadequate and error-ridden models.

Building an AI solution, requires a deep appreciation of machine learning architecture which means that true Data Scientists are likely to have a PHD-level qualification. With such skills they can appreciate the broader issues, address error and bias and potential problems with the system.

However they must be wary of:

- Aiming for increased automation over the genuine benefits to the company;
- Delivering a practical solution;
- Producing a solution that is explainable.

Automation

Machine Learning can produce exciting results and I have worked with third parties selling solutions with the view of total automation: model build, learn and re-build. This is attractive but the user should remember to consider the issues of error and bias. If you turn on such a device without addressing such issues – or providing a mechanism to spot when they arise or become significant, you are likely to be jeopardizing the future success of the business. With a short term loan, the outcome and learning process is quick. However, traditional, longer term loans and revolving products take years to mature and irreparable damage could have been done by AI before the mistake is identified.

Practicality

The ability to implement a model has always been important and I experienced an international modelling team who were amazing statisticians but failed to have one of their solutions implemented within the two years they operated. The main issue was that they didn't consider the operating environments. Modern tools weren't available for deployment and so when they built neural networks, the models couldn't be used in legacy production systems.

The modern issues tend to be slightly different. Firstly the Data Scientist should check the availability of the data. It may well be in the modeling sample, but is it available in the live environment? An example of this might be student data captured by the compiling organization who then provided it anonymised to the Data Scientist. However the lender may not be able to or have previously asked the question – or validate the response if they can.

Data protection has added another level to this area of concern. When LenderA first started, they obtained detailed FaceBook data without asking for consent. Initially they didn't need to. It wasn't long after this became public, that the access was removed.

Explainable

There are two reasons why the models should make sense. Firstly, nonsense variables can creep into a model. The problem is that we have a sample of the whole population and there will be errors (statistics is all about errors and understanding them). As a result, spurious things can happen, and variables can appear predictive simply because of the bias in the sample. Therefore knowing and sanity checking the variables and their contribution to the decision is important. Some machine learning solutions convert the complex algorithm into something that a human can understand.

Regulators around the world are already grappling with the problem of how to ensure that "scorecards" are fair and non-discriminatory. This is the second reason why the model should be explainable. If you can't demonstrate to the regulator that your decision system doesn't discriminate—and doesn't use any data that's not allowed – then the business is likely to be fined. It might not happen in your country yet, but it is coming, and fast.

Little Data

The desire to build AI solutions is both strong within the data science world and investors. The latter want real discrimination over their rivals and know that data can provide this. However this desire can lead to over-complication and, as a result, worse performance for the company.

I have always been a champion of the **KISS** (Keep It Simple Stupid) principle and this definitely applies to scorecard development. FICO used to recommend a minimum of 1,500 Goods, Bads and Rejects for a model build. The following is a rough guide that I know a number of developers follow:

Model type	Minimum number of Bads
Neural Network	10,000
Logistic Regression	1,500
Linear Regression	1,000
Weight of Evidence	500
Bayesian model	50
Expert model	0

Figure 1: Suggested minimum sample sizes by modeling approach

Logistic regression is favoured by the traditional scorecard developer because of the anticipated exponential increase in risk as quality deteriorates. It also provides a better fit when considering dummy variables, however regression provides the correlation coefficients giving the relationship between the independent and dependent (Good/Bad) variable and we know that the larger the sample (principally, the number of Bads) the smaller the spread of outcomes (errors). Building a regression model on small samples therefore runs the risk of identifying and overstating these coefficients. The result is over-fitting: a model that works well on the sample but will be suboptimal on future samples.

This problem is exacerbated by machine learning approaches, because it isn't just about the final model but "binning" the data as well—grouping attributes sensibly to provide more robustness. If this isn't scrutinized, it can result in super-errors—where the attributes have been combined because of spurious outcomes, thereby boosting the error. All of which means that AI models must have very large datasets (possibly tens of thousands of Bads) and intense scrutiny of the variables and variable construction.

Conclusion

If the data just isn't there, do not fool yourself into thinking you can use a more advanced technique than is justified. And of course, don't go looking for additional data (principally Bads) from samples that aren't representative: too young (resulting in a mis-classification issue), or too old (being a representative data issue) or from a different product.

A simple model that is understood, will nearly always out perform a complex model that isn't. Learning should be a continuous process and by starting simple, you will learn from the model so that the next iteration is better, and the next better still.

Big Data, Little Data, and Data Science is an edited version of a chapter in Credit Scoring: Principles and Practicalities, fourth edition, and is available now.

Here is a sample of feedback from Windsor's original course: The Ten Tools of Credit Scoring. The company in brackets is where the student worked at the time.

"If you want to know what credit analysts should do, go on this course."
Simon Lowings (Vauxhall Finance)

"Learned a huge amount and enjoyed the course"
Tracy Gorman (Bank of Scotland)

"Very good course. Murray has so much information the course could do with being 4 days!"
Luke Reynolds (NatWest)

"Very well put together. A worthwhile course to attend."
Alan North (MBNA)

"The course met all my objectives and I have learnt a lot that I will take back to put to work in my job."
Rebecca Kirkman (The Associates)

"A very enjoyable course. The game is an excellent way to put learning into practice to enable you to see the fruits of your labour - or error or your ways."
Jo Brown (Birmingham Midshires)

"The information will definitely help in applying these techniques in the work place."
Linda Higgs (RBS)

"I learnt much more information relating to my work…it was great to learn some very valuable tools"
Barbara Plowright (GMAC)

"Murray was excellent at putting across ideas and covering questions"
Neil Lewis (Bradford & Bingley)

"Really beneficial… there are similar courses available, but none provide the same insights or depth of understanding."
Julie Hill (Birmingham Midshires)

"Very helpful in allowing me to probe into the mystique of credit scoring and its contribution to our business."
Robin Bulloch (GE Capital Woodchester)

"Tool number 11 – Attend this course! Thoroughly recommended."
Tom Paxton (Bank of Scotland)

"This course is bang on what I needed for my job!"
Russell Benton (NatWest)

"A good blend of information, practical advice and enjoyment."
Dave Manns (Paragon)

"Enjoyed being able to relate to real situations. Should be easily applied to the workplace."
Matt Howells (NatWest)

Murray Bailey has been focused on retail financial services for over 30 years, specializing in Credit Risk Management. He has acted as a Chief Risk Officer on a number of occasions, most significantly at GE Capital Bank.

Having graduated with a First Class Honours Degree in Physics and Part III of the Mathematics Tripos from Cambridge University, Murray joined Welbeck Finance and built a methodology for scorecard development before commencing scorecard builds. After a short time he became Assistant Credit Risk Director at Citibank Savings before joining HFC Bank at Credit Risk Director. In 1997 he established his training and consultancy business and has since worked with many of the lenders in the UK.

He is the author and editor of a number of text books and spent a year as the editor of Credit Risk International. He is also the author of mystery-thrillers, details of which can be found at murraybaileybooks.com

Murray now acts mainly as an author, NED and credit risk advisor.